$/ 7.00

Making *Amends*

◇

Finding a new freedom

Stories from AA Grapevine

D1371904

BOOKS PUBLISHED BY AA GRAPEVINE, INC.

The Language of the Heart (& eBook)
The Best of the Grapevine Volume I (eBook)
The Best of Bill (& eBook)
Thank You for Sharing
Spiritual Awakenings (& eBook)
I Am Responsible: The Hand of AA
The Home Group: Heartbeat of AA (eBook)
Emotional Sobriety — The Next Frontier (& eBook)
Spiritual Awakenings II (& eBook)
In Our Own Words: Stories of Young AAs in Recovery (& eBook)
Beginners' Book (& eBook)
Voices of Long-Term Sobriety (& eBook)
A Rabbit Walks Into A Bar
Step by Step — Real AAs, Real Recovery (& eBook)
Emotional Sobriety II — The Next Frontier (& eBook)
Young & Sober (& eBook)
Into Action (& eBook)
Happy, Joyous & Free (& eBook)
One on One (& eBook)
No Matter What (& eBook)
Grapevine Daily Quote Book (& eBook)
Sober & Out (& eBook)
Forming True Partnerships (& eBook)
Our Twelve Traditions ((& eBook)

IN SPANISH
El lenguaje del corazón
Lo mejor de Bill (& eBook)
El grupo base: Corazón de AA
Lo mejor de La Viña
Felices, alegres y libres (& eBook)
Un día a la vez (& eBook)

IN FRENCH
Le langage du coeur
Les meilleurs articles de Bill
Le Groupe d'attache: Le battement du coeur des AA
En tête à tête (& eBook)
Heureux, joyeux et libres (& eBook)

Making
Amends

◇

Finding a new freedom

Stories from AA Grapevine

AAGRAPEVINE, Inc.
New York, New York
WWW.AAGRAPEVINE.ORG

Copyright © 2017 by AA Grapevine, Inc.
475 Riverside Drive
New York, New York 10115
All rights reserved

May not be reprinted in full or in part, except in short passages for purposes
of review or comment, without written permission from the publisher.

AA and Alcoholics Anonymous are registered trademarks of AA World Services, Inc.

Twelve Steps copyright © AA World Services, Inc.; reprinted with permission

ISBN: 978-1-938413-16-2

Printed in Canada

AA Preamble

Alcoholics Anonymous is a fellowship of men and women
who share their experience, strength and hope
with each other that they may solve their common problem
and help others to recover from alcoholism.

The only requirement for membership is a desire to stop drinking.
There are no dues or fees for AA membership;
we are self-supporting through our own contributions.
AA is not allied with any sect, denomination, politics, organization
or institution; does not wish to engage in any controversy,
neither endorses nor opposes any causes.

Our primary purpose is to stay sober
and help other alcoholics to achieve sobriety.

©*AA Grapevine, Inc.*

Contents

CHAPTER ONE

Step Eight: We Don't Rush Into Amends

The effects of Step Nine on our lives and others' will last a long time—even a lifetime—so paving our way via Step Eight is vital

CHAPTER TWO

Addressing the Past with Our Wounded Parents

We find peace after all with the ones who witnessed our beginnings

CHAPTER THREE

Offering Our Amends to the Children We Love

Tender or tough, Step Nine offers both parents and children a new birth day

CHAPTER FOUR

Bringing Our Amends Back Home

When our addiction has rippled through our family, healing can too

CHAPTER FIVE
Exes: Finally Divorced From the Pain

The guilt and shame of past relationships can still run—and ruin—
a life, until Step Nine changes everything

CHAPTER SIX
Where the Guilt Runs Deep, So Can the Peace

Nothing is more painful than sitting humbly before a victim of your
crime ... except avoiding that day

CHAPTER SEVEN
Active Alcoholism and Money: An Amends Waiting to Happen

A brave reconciliation with our financial failures is an investment
like no other

CHAPTER EIGHT

Finally Reaching Out to Those We So Often Kept at Bay

Our friends and coworkers, who were always close at hand, easy targets for our addictive behavior, are now recipients of our amends

Welcome

"We are going to know a new freedom and a new happiness.
We will not regret the past nor wish to shut the door on it. We
will comprehend the word serenity and we will know peace.
No matter how far down the scale we have gone, we will see
how our experience can benefit others."

— Alcoholics Anonymous

*M*aking Amends features 55 candid, firsthand stories from Grapevine magazine of AA members' experiences with Step Nine of the AA program. The book is divided into eight main chapters, including sections on Step Eight, parents, children, family members, exes, special cases, financial, and finally, friends and coworkers.

Step Nine is a challenging, life-changing practice that requires preparation, so the book begins with a chapter of Step Eight experiences. In "Ready to Sweep," the book's first story, the writer leaves no doubt why these Steps are necessary. "When I was an active alcoholic, I caused physical, mental and spiritual damage to people," writes member Gary T. In our understandable hesitance to dive into these most grownup of Steps, we sometimes express the idea that our fellows are tired of hearing our apologies, which is where our sponsors point out that when we back our car into a fence, we don't turn to it and say, "I'm sorry," we take out our hammer and nails. We make a mend. In "Learning How to Forgive," D.W.R. realizes what had frozen his emotions, even in making amends: "I wasn't forgiving them for not forgiving me."

Parents often top the list of those harmed by our addiction, and in Chapter 2's story "Making Amends," C.M.'s mother welcomes his by assuring him that, "You do make amends to me each time you reach out to a newcomer." In Chapter 3, we see that our vulnerable children are too often the victims of our drinking as well. In "The Luckiest Mom,"

Pat T. had given her daughter up for adoption, and when it occurs to her to make her amends, she is miraculously able to do so in person.

The ravages of our disease ripple clearly through our families, and in Keith W.'s article "A Quiet Hatred," in Chapter 4, his amends took the form of a racial reconciliation that seemed impossible. In Chapter 5, our exes, once our loves, are so often bound to us by negatives, thanks to our alcoholic behavior. In "Scene of the Crime," Kit K. found enough peace in the quiet of a volcano crater to make a face-to-face amends to her once violent ex, remembering her sponsor saying, "Courage is fear that has said its prayers."

Garden variety fears fade in comparison to how we feel when the amends we must make are the survivors of those who did not survive our alcoholism. In the Chapter 6 story "The Amends I Most Dreaded to Make," member D.S. reaches out to the beloved sister of the pedestrian he ran down who eventually died from her injuries, and is taken in as "a dear, real brother." In Chapter 7, we're reminded that money doesn't mix with alcoholism, and the financial collision that often occurs leaves scars deeper than debts. In "Tax Returns," an anonymous author writes that the bond between the amends-maker and the tax collector was "the silent work of a Higher Power."

And in the book's final chapter, we see that friends and coworkers, some of whom have been our drinking buddies, have invariably been in the vicinity as we drank, close enough to be harmed. Clearing our side of the street with them wins us back our self-esteem as well. As B.F. writes about her relationship with a dear friend in "Open and Honest," "I had to be good to myself and stop dragging the past with me whenever I encountered Lynne."

As the powerful stories in this book illustrate, we can count on Step Nine to mark, as our co-founder Bill W. wrote, "the beginning of the end of isolation from our fellows and from God."

CHAPTER ONE

Step Eight: We Don't Rush Into Amends

—◇—

The effects of Step Nine on our lives and others'
will last a long time—even a lifetime—so paving our
way via Step Eight is vital

"**D**riven by a hundred forms of fear," says the Big Book, "self-delusion, self-seeking, and self-pity, we step on the toes of our fellows and they retaliate." With Steps Eight and Nine, we heal those relationships, as well as our primary relationship with ourselves. It's only after working Step Nine that the inspiring AA Promises can be expected.

No matter how eager we are to clear our side of the street with everyone, we are advised to prepare well first. And we do that through working the other seven Steps. In the story "The Mending Process," later on in the book, Corinne H. describes the chaos she created as she rushed headlong into Step Nine, "without benefit of sponsor or sanity."

In this chapter's story "From Our Fellows and From God," member W.H. writes about the many fears that can cause us to hesitate before Steps Eight and Nine. "What will she think?" or "What will he say?" Followed by our famous, "What an order! I can't go through with it." But to the writer, "Fear of losing my sobriety overrode my fear of losing someone's goodwill." W.H. also wisely points out that Step Eight "provides a time of calm reflection before we get down to the actual amends-making task."

The anonymous writer in the story "The Eighth Step," describes "this great life": "I have found, to my great joy, that if I work on Eight and

Nine and keep the emphasis on my relationships with others, these Steps actually do bring about the ultimate amends to me—a happy, sober day-to-day life that brims over with gladness, happiness, good fortune, and all that I could wish for."

Ready to Sweep
August 2015

When I was an active alcoholic, I caused physical, mental and spiritual damage to people. And as my drinking became more destructive, I isolated and alienated myself from others even more than usual, in an attempt to drink and drug without interruption or negative criticism. I'd then be overwhelmed with fear, shame, guilt and remorse. My self-loathing would spill over into all my relationships—the few that still remained, that is.

The Eighth Step gave me the toolbox I needed to explore these relationships more deeply. It enabled me to pinpoint those individuals whom I had harmed. And even if I was not actually ready to make direct amends to certain people, I was able to begin by writing out an amends list and praying for the willingness.

As I worked through my list, the essential question for me, as it says in the "Twelve and Twelve," was: "Whom have I harmed and in what ways?" I was tempted to recall and list the ways these people had hurt me. In all honesty, there was perhaps harm on both sides. But I needed to focus on the harm I had produced. The Eighth Step does not depend on the character defects and shortcomings of others. I had to admit and acknowledge my own character defects and shortcomings. I needed to focus on "sweeping my side of the street."

When feelings of defensiveness began to emerge, I remembered that these individuals needed my forgiveness just as much as I needed theirs. But whether they recognized that need was not the issue. If I were to be serious about mending broken relationships, and I certainly was, I needed to let go of my resentments and, simultaneously, to forgive others. The following questions were helpful to me as I worked on my Eighth Step:

1) How was I bad-tempered because of my drinking?

2) Did I avoid friends and family as a result of my obsession?

3) What damage did I produce by letting my self-will run riot? These helped me gain valuable insights and discover other people to add to my list.

As I continued on my Eighth Step journey, it became apparent that I did much damage to myself as well. And it dawned on me that the most effective amends that I could make to myself was to stay sober and practice the Steps to the best of my ability. And if I keep not drinking just for today, I won't drink for the rest of my life.

In early sobriety, I would never have contemplated making the first move toward making an amend. But now I'm attempting to discern and apply the will of God in my life. I now take responsibility for my sobriety and for my relationships. Taking such a risk has become a possibility thanks to the Steps and my support network in the rooms of AA. The Eighth Step has given me the ability to maintain and develop a deep intimacy and involvement with significant others in my life. It also gives me emotional and spiritual balance.

Gary T.
Poughkeepsie, New York

From Our Fellows and From God
February 1986

A re you the type of person who makes lists? There are a lot of us around. We make lists of household items, groceries and toiletries; of things to do today, tomorrow and over the weekend; of holidays, vacations and activities for special events.

At many Step discussion meetings in my area, I hear my fellow AAs share their fear upon reaching the Eighth Step. Usually, it's the fear of the impending Ninth Step confrontation with those they have harmed. "What will she think?" or "What will he say?" followed by our famous "What an order! I can't go through with it." Eventually, I was asking the same questions and entertaining similar fears. However, something had to be done because old-timers said that their sobriety depended on how successfully they continued to practice all twelve of the Steps. So I began putting a list together. Fear of losing my sobriety overrode my fear of losing someone's goodwill.

Naturally, at the head of the list I put my own name, right? No. I was far too used to being first in the universe, far too self-centered. But didn't I hurt myself more than anybody else by my drinking? Perhaps, but amends to myself began the moment I put the cork in the bottle. At least, that's the way I came to see it.

My immediate family was high on my list. First my parents, whom I had long blamed for certain deficiencies in my makeup (in addition to my alcoholism); my brother and sisters who I felt had always made unreasonable demands on me.

There were the stores where I had begun a history of petty thievery during my teens. Small thefts, but they totaled up to a pretty penny.

There were couples whose marriages, already a bit shaky, I had done nothing to help. Fact is, I contributed to the grounds for at least one divorce.

There were jobs where I cheated employers of their fair due, as well as setting a very poor example by my drunkenness.

There were romantic love objects, persons used and then tossed aside.

And how many were victims of my big-shotism—people I promised to help find living quarters or jobs through my "connections"? What connections?

That's a broad outline of my first serious approach to making amends. What did I do about it all? How do you make amends to somebody who has moved to you-know-not-where? How do you return stolen goods to a now-defunct store?

Our founding fathers wisely provided the Eighth Step as a means of collecting our wits, of charting our course as we prepare for a journey that might well prove to be stormy. It is a course where I might find it impossible, due to circumstances, to make amends, but not impossible to include my willingness on my list. To become willing. The Step is also about that, isn't it?

The Eighth Step provides a time of calm reflection before we get down to the actual amends-making task. As the "Twelve and Twelve" says, "It is the beginning of the end of isolation from our fellows and from God."

W. H.
New York, New York

From At Wit's End
June 2001

Heard at Meetings: "When you make a mistake, make amends immediately. It's easier to eat crow while it's still warm."

Susan C.
Richmond, Virginia

8 1/2
October 1986

As I continue to live each 24 hours in the Fellowship of Alcoholics Anonymous and attempt to practice its principles in all my affairs, one Step seems to play an increasingly important role in my life and in my relationships with others. This quiet but potent Step is Step Eight: "Made a list of all persons we had harmed, and became willing to make amends to them all."

Many people, myself included, tend to lump Steps Eight and Nine together. By doing this, I never really achieved even a glimmer of the humility and love that Step Eight has to offer. Being a person of impatient actions, I was off and running on Step Nine with a simple list of names tightly grasped in my sweaty hand and a bad case of false humility to go along with it. Needless to say, I came home each evening with a battered sense of justice and my tail tucked underneath me.

As usual, I did not read all the words contained in the Step, and just as I had done in Step One, I read only the first half before jumping to the next Step. The resulting self-induced pain has, however, taught me much about myself and the principles of this simple program.

Going back to Step Eight, I read the words at last, "... became willing to make amends to them all." As I began to absorb what was being said to me, and as I reviewed the first seven Steps leading up to this one, it suddenly became clear what the message was for me and what the hasty mistake of impatient interpretation had cost me in serenity. The word "identify" held the key to my success with this Step. To become willing means to become willing to identify myself in others. I had been using Step Eight not as preparation for Step Nine, which is the carrying out of that willingness, but as a hiding place for my own real fear of my true shortcomings. The purpose of Step Eight for me is not to hide but to identify. In order not to identify, I either condemned or forgave as if I were some kind of standard for comparison. In this Step I receive the humility to "identify," to see myself in others and to share their burdens and difficulties by sharing myself. In this Step I truly join the human race. My identification becomes my freedom— freedom from fear and anger. When I can identify my own shortcomings in another, the battleground between us is removed.

I cannot make an amends when I am still condemning or forgiving myself or the one I am making amends to, because of the judgment this implies. I have always found condemnation to be a lonely road and have always found forgiveness to be a confusing and impossible task. When I forgive someone I guess what I really mean to say is that I admit I judge others. Forgiving and condemning are God's business, not mine. Only he has the mercy to judge and to accept at the same time. My job is to achieve enough humility to see myself in others and to accept both myself and others, by identifying. The willingness to make amends will grow from this act of love. When I become "willing to make amends to them all" I am saying to them, "your pain is my pain; when I hurt you, I hurt myself; I will try not to hurt you anymore."

When I have achieved this kind of willingness to identify, my Higher Power has always set up my amends and allowed both of us to grow from the love involved in such an act.

E. C.
Bowling Green, Kentucky

Learning How to Forgive
(From Around the Tables)
January 1973

Over a period of many 24 hours, I have experienced many versions of the Eighth and Ninth Steps of the AA guide to recovery. As the chemical fog lifted, I endeavored to cope with the havoc caused by my insanity. One particular problem persisted: While I had made financial restitution, I couldn't grasp an approach toward the emotional amends which I felt necessary.

The answer, as I now see it, is that I had to learn the true meaning of forgiveness. My prayers for aid in amends were getting nowhere because I hadn't forgiven.

"After all, can't they see how changed I am? Why don't they accept me? What's wrong? Do I have to crawl before them? Here I am not drinking, and they don't seem impressed by the change." Maybe you hear a hint of a wee little resentment or self-pride. Right—I wasn't forgiving them for not forgiving me.

I could pray and pray, but no forgiveness came. Now, I'm praying that I weed out all the subtle "unforgiveness" that has been growing for lo, these many years. Once I have truly, through prayer, forgiven any and all for real and imagined injuries, I'll be forgiven. When I have really forgiven, then the flow starts towards me, and then the amends can be made. For me, at least, I have lots of forgiving to do before I can make amends.

D. W. R.
Detroit, Michigan

The Eighth Step
(From Around the Tables)
October 1977

I have, of late, participated in a succession of discussions centering on the Eighth Step. I regard this Step as the easiest but perhaps the most subtle in the program. It requires only that I make a list of people I have harmed and become willing to make amends to them all. Unlike Step Five, Eight does not require that I seek out a companion and unload it on him. It does not require searching my soul or being humble—only making a list and becoming willing. Step Nine requires some damn bold action, so it is very different from, though obviously dependent on, Step Eight.

The Eighth Step relates to people other than me. Unquestionably, it points outward and not inward. Many of us feel anger about this position and protest, "I didn't hurt anyone else but me. I figure I have to make amends to me." The phrasing may vary, but the idea is always the same: "make amends to me." Frankly, I think this is so much garbage. It's one of the "old ideas" the Big Book advises us to discard—namely, selfishness. If the founders had meant Eight and Nine to be directed at themselves, they would have so stated in plain English.

But here's an AA paradox: I have found, to my great joy, that if I work on Eight and Nine and keep the emphasis on my relationships with others, these Steps actually do bring about the ultimate amends to me—a happy, sober day-to-day life that brims over with gladness, happiness, good fortune and all that I could wish for. It's far better to work on the Steps the way the Big Book and the "Twelve and Twelve" suggest than to risk losing this great life.

Anonymous

Real Men Don't Make Amends—Do They?
October 1984

Many times at meetings, I've heard something like "I did so and so. Do I have to make amends?" Or "A man never says he's sorry." Or "I'm just going to make a living amends by behaving myself." Or "What good does it do?"

Sound familiar? It sure does to me. I've had all those negative attitudes at one time or another during my sobriety. It seems as though considering amends removed everything positive from my outlook on life. Then, the excuses started exaggerating themselves, and another chance to become a better person through our program slipped away. How many of those chances did I miss because false pride engendered a negative attitude toward amends? Almost all of them.

Now, thanks to God, good strong sponsorship and a great AA group, my attitude regarding amends is no longer negative. I've learned to make an amends that is a positive experience, not just putting a check mark on a list to fill a square. Just filling a square is not growth; it is just filling a square, the way I did when I was drinking. Growth is characterized by an identifiable change in attitude for the better. It is apparent in the way we conduct ourselves, in the way we express ourselves, in our actions. Fortunately, it comes in many ways.

The growth I have experienced through amends began when I found out exactly what an amends is not. Much to my surprise, it is not crawling on my belly or becoming a doormat or belittling myself. I no longer have to try to act responsible for events I had no control over. Did you ever try to alter events that took place when you were not even there? I don't need to justify myself or make excuses. Making amends means taking sole responsibility for all my actions and letting others have the responsibility for theirs.

An amends is taking the episodes of my life that haunt me and laying them to rest, finally. It allows me to walk down my side of the street with my head up, unafraid of anyone I may encounter. It makes it possible for me to anticipate life instead of hiding from it. Life is to be lived, not battled or avoided.

An amends is allowing those I abused in my disease to participate in my recovery. I owe them that, and more important, I owe myself that. I believe that each time I committed an offense against another person, in reality I committed a far greater offense against myself. The offenses against others pale in significance when compared with the internal havoc I wreaked within myself.

I've found that mistreating others is really a two-part deal. First, I go against my values by telling myself it is OK to commit a wrong against someone else. My ethics and morals both say this is wrong, yet when I take over the management of my life, I tend to override any good sense I ever had. The pursuit of a fleeting moment's excitement becomes more important than living up to my own standards. Each time I did that, I gave a piece of myself away. I believe my self-esteem when I got here was on the minus side of the page because I had given so many pieces of myself away.

Second, I committed the wrong against another person. Therefore, each time I was harmful to others, I gave that piece of myself to them, thus giving away control of my actions and thinking. That was certainly evident by the pains I went to in order to avoid those I had wronged. I even had to change my route to the washroom at work, taking a longer, more devious path. Fear. Guilt. Hiding. Have you ever avoided going someplace you really wanted to go, because you knew one of your "victims" would be there too? Not a fun way to live.

Upon sobering up, joining AA and setting out on the "Road of Happy Destiny," I discovered a new strength within. That strength has allowed me to make my amends, and as a result, I've experienced some of the most profound and moving moments of my sobriety. Some really marvelous people reentered my life because of my amends attempts, and we are closer today than before. You see, prior to the amends, I had never stopped to really look at them, to put myself in their place, to empathize with them, to consider their importance in my life, to just be polite. I found some really good folks where I had previously seen small, inferior, bothersome persons.

Each person did one big thing for me. They all returned the small pieces of myself I had left in their charge, thus participating in my recovery by assisting me to become whole again. The more I was able to follow the Big Book in making my amends, the better I felt. It astounds me that those I wronged are able to contribute so much to my recovery. Once I discovered this, I began to seek them out more fervently, and my amends really began to enhance my sobriety. I am still amazed at God's power to put the wreck I was back together.

It has been eight years since my first bumbling attempts at amends, and I'm pretty much whole again. All the negative feelings I used to associate with Step Nine are gone. My Higher Power has allowed me to experience our wonderful way of life to the fullest, and I want more of it.

There is yet one piece of myself still in the care of another, and I am looking forward to going home for that visit in a few months. Thanks to God, our program, my sponsor and my group, I have all the tickets I need for a very rewarding excursion into a few moments of my past. I left part of myself and someone I need there. I'm going back to get them.

N. D.
Omaha, Nebraska

How Willing Would You Be?
August 1991

Although my body walked, my spirit crawled out of the room where I had just completed my Fifth Step. I was so sick of myself and my character defects that I was totally willing to take the Sixth and Seventh Steps.

Then came Step Eight. The first part of this Step was easy. The Big Book told me that I had made my list when I made my inventory, so I took my list of persons I had harmed from my Fourth Step.

The second part of this Step was not so easy. "Willing," it said. There's that word again; the Big Book and the "Twelve and Twelve" seem to use that word a lot. It's written in Step Three, again emphasized in Step Six, and here it is again in Step Eight. As I looked my list over, there were many amends I was willing to make, as I could see where I had been childish, selfish and self-centered. But there were some that brought back hurts so deep I was not willing to make amends then— and I seriously doubted if I ever would be. The words from the Big Book kept playing through my head, "We have emphasized willingness as being indispensable." I knew that, but I still wasn't willing.

Reading over the part on Step Eight in the Big Book, I saw I wasn't unique; earlier AAs had evidently been like me. This was apparent when I read the line that says, "There are probably still some misgivings," and again when I read, "If we haven't the will to do this, we ask until it comes." (Ask God, of course.)

I kept praying about the difficult amends while I was making other amends, and it seemed like every meeting I attended during that time was on the Eighth Step. In one of these meetings, I heard someone share her experience. She had been willing to make all her amends but one. In talking to her sponsor about it, the sponsor put it like this: If your program depended upon this one amends—that is, if you made this amends you would stay sober, and if you didn't make it you would drink again—how willing would you be then?

Hearing that, and reading again about going to any length, brought me the willingness I had been praying for—at least on all but one. Deep in my heart I knew it would take a miracle for the willingness to come for that one, and when the exact moment was right, God gave me the willingness so suddenly that it was like a physical force slammed into me. Once again, God was right on time, not a minute too early or a second too late.

Since I've been in the program, I've been told countless times that if I will take care of the possible, God will handle the impossible. Countless times I've witnessed this to be true.

It's been over two-and-a-half years since all this happened, and I'm still sober. I can only say it's because of God and not me, for the part I played has been so small in comparison to God's part. I thank God for AA, and for the fact that, just for today, I'm still willing.

Robi M.
Edmond, Oklahoma

CHAPTER TWO

Addressing the Past with Our Wounded Parents

◇

We find peace after all with the ones who witnessed our beginnings

O ur parents were rarely far away when we took our first drink and, as our addiction kicked in, their natural concern turned to worry and often crippling dread. Whatever their own challenges, and however our parents' behavior affected—even afflicted—us, it's our responsibility to clean up our side of the street.

And with our sponsor's help, we set out to do just that. In the story "At My Father's Grave," Ed L. recalls how, after 30 years of hatred, he was able to make amends to his dad, two decades after his death. In another story, member Smoochie ultimately found "The Dad I Could Love," despite having his amends greeted at first by hearing "nasty, ugly things" from him. In the article "What I Do Owe," Leon A. made his amends in the form of forgiveness, standing before his father's unmarked grave, making it possible for Leon to put away the pistol with the .38 slug he had waiting for him at home. And it took 40 years after her mother was buried for the writer Anonymous to make "My Last Amend," not a minute too late.

It soon becomes very clear who benefits most from including our parents in Step Nine—another gift of AA.

My Last Amend
June 2014

S
ome things take time. Some things take a lot of time—like 40 years. The last thing on my amends list that I was just unable to face, I finally did. I've been blessed to learn in this program that my life is rich because of the people in it. I was able to do this last amend, not with my husband or children or any relatives who knew my mother, but with members of my sponsorship family. Three women took me to her gravesite an hour away from where I live, which I hadn't visited since the day I buried her 40 years ago.

My mother had committed suicide the same day that I had an abortion. She was a poor lost soul who had no one who loved her in a healthy way, and no hope. She was 52 years old and all alone in the world, wandering constantly and never finding any peace. She could not break the chains that bound her. The day of her burial there was nothing that could dull my pain. It was the worst day of my life. I remember drinking martini after martini, but I couldn't get drunk.

My mother gave me away when I was six months old. She was a waitress at the time. I did get the opportunity to ask her once, when I met her on the road, why she had given me away. Her answer was, "Because they could give you a better life than I could." I didn't understand what a sacrifice she had made, and how right that move was, until I got sober and became a parent myself and arrived at the place where I realized that there was nothing I wouldn't do for my amazing children.

My boyfriend at the time was married. Abortion had become legal six months prior to that in the state where we lived. So I found myself waiting with four other women, wearing used hospital gowns in a dismal hospital room. We sat there whimpering, full of sorrow and despair, of which I had a double dose. We were treated like the scum of the earth. My situation was horrid: I didn't want to bring a child into my miserable life and have to give him or her away like my biological mother had done with me.

I arrived at my mother's funeral in a wheelchair and nearly threw myself on the ground as the white coffin was lowered into the ground. That day I met my biological siblings and went on a two-year binge with my brother and his wife. When I was 90 days sober, I Twelfth-Stepped her. That was the end of her marriage, but the beginning of her sobriety.

I hadn't been able to touch that pain again until this past July, which was the 40-year anniversary of my mother's death. She had hated red and black, so I wore white, brought pink roses, and cried from the bottom of my soul while my sponsees held me and we all prayed. I brought her a photo of my beautiful husband and three children and gave her my sobriety medallion. I told her about the amazing life I've had and that she had done the right thing. I told her how sorry I was for not being able to do more for her, for not being there to help her more, for not visiting all this time. I know she forgave me.

I touched the pain, lived through it, and was freed. Like everything I've done since I crawled into this program so many moons ago, I could not, and did not have to, do it alone.

Anonymous

At My Father's Grave
March 2013

Here I was, sober only six months, and I was standing over my biological father's grave. My adopted father and his younger brother were there beside me. We were in the cemetery of my childhood home of Roanoke, Virginia, which was a long way from where I live in Wrightwood, California. But that's where following good orderly direction had led me.

My father died back in 1988, and on this cold overcast November day in 2005, I was working my AA Ninth Step with him. He'd led a less-than-exemplary life, having been arrested for lack of child-support when my mother died, and was buried on her 50th birthday in 1970. But then, so had I led a less-than-exemplary life that, to this day, only my sponsors and I are fully aware of, thank God! So how could I possibly make amends to someone who had been dead nearly two decades?

Troy B., my first sponsor, answered: "Simple but not easy!" He said I was to write a three-part letter. In the first part, I would forgive my dad. In the second part, I would ask his forgiveness. And, in the third part, I was to describe how my life would change as a result of all this forgiveness. I still don't understand this present life or the afterlife well enough to know how the first two parts worked, although I did what I was asked to do, with simple faith. It's the third part that I better understand, now having exercised it over the past few years.

After 30 years of hating the man who had seemingly caused my family and me so much harm, it came naturally for me to bad-mouth him to anyone who would listen (and some who wouldn't). Thirty years of habitually thinking he was the source of all my woes didn't disappear overnight. That's the beauty of the third part of the letter! For in that part, I wrote that I no longer have the right to denigrate someone whom I've forgiven! I can no longer dwell on my father's poor behavior, which I've come to understand is, itself, poor behavior.

When my mind wanders back to that deep, dark cave I'd excavated over those 30 years, I remind myself about the third part of that letter, and my living amends. I'm now able to turn away from that strangely inviting, dark resentment, much like Victor E. habitually turns away from that yawning blackhole of a barroom door that unerringly and unsuccessfully invites him in time and time again for a drink.

Ed L.
Wrightwood, California

The Road From Reno
September 2014

As the plane took off my father asked, "Is it going to bother you if I use these two free drink coupons on this flight?" He wasn't going to drink them, but they were free and he was a frugal man. I was just about two years sober and the last thing he wanted to do was to put my sobriety at risk. At my first AA birthday he had asked my sponsor, "How much do I owe you?" That was the only way he knew how to say thank you. We are not wealthy by any means, and I had lived on my own for more than 20 years, but he was grateful for what AA had done for me and my family.

This trip was part of the process of making amends to my parents. My mother had asked me if I'd help drive a car back from Reno, Nevada. She had purchased it from her brother's estate. I said yes, of course. I had my wife's OK to go; she knew I needed to do it (thank God for Al-Anon).

In Reno everything happens around the casino. My uncle's wife was part of a group of older ladies who ate breakfast in the casino, went back for lunch, and then, after a nap, went back for dinner to play a bit of keno. So I had to spend quite a bit of time in the casino. To my surprise, I never had a thought of drinking.

I escaped the temptations of the "Biggest Little City in the World," and we drove back to our hometown of Memphis, Tennessee in Mom's new car. It was a long trip, and I drove the biggest part of it. It was the least I could do for my parents; after all, they had rescued me time and time again. I even had them smuggling in food on the weekend while I was in the penal farm, or as I lovingly called it, the Shelby County Country Club, where I did a one to three-year sentence for crimes related to my drinking. In other words, I owed them a lot more than I could ever pay back by driving from Reno to Memphis.

My father and I had those frank and honest talks about what I had done and about how I could make it right. We both had admitted our faults, and I had done what was necessary to clean my side of the street. Of course, me staying sober was the biggest part as far as he was concerned. I was very grateful to have been able to get that one under my belt.

As we were driving back from Reno, Dad and I were in the front seat and Mom was in the back seat. Everything was just rolling along; life was good. I had talked to my wife and son back home and they were eagerly anticipating my return, all as a result of the new lease on life AA had given me. As the conversation in the front seat turned to the past, I thought maybe this was the right time to have that frank and honest talk with Mom about all of my faults and past misdeeds—to clear the air, so to speak. It seemed to be the perfect opportunity to make "direct amends" to her, so I launched into some of the details of my past transgressions, and said that, if I could, I'd go back and redo things. I added how much I regretted doing those things.

Then I looked into the mirror, and I saw the look in her eyes. I knew immediately that these things I was bringing up caused her to remember the dark days of the decades before I entered AA. I could see the pain that I was putting her through as she remembered those times when she didn't know if her baby was dead or alive. Not to mention the time when her youngest son was sentenced to the state penitentiary for the crimes he had committed while under the influence. And did I need to make her remember the time when she brought my two children from my first marriage to visit me at Christmas, in a gymnasium inside that penitentiary? Those were just a handful of the situations I had forced her to endure. I knew immediately I had no right to bring up those painful memories. Trying to right the wrongs of my past, I was causing her more pain.

Thank God for good sponsorship, because Jack and I had discussed the Ninth Step and what it says about making "direct amends" to people, "except when to do so would injure them or others." The rule of thumb is: hard on us, easy on others. I don't have the right to hurt those people any more, and I have to bear the burden on my own two shoulders.

With Mom I have continued to make those amends by doing whatever I could to be of service to her. For many years, I called her every day and would go by whenever she needed something, or just whenever I thought I could help in any way—even when she didn't ask. Before my father died a few years ago, I was able to help Mom take care of him and make the arrangements for his funeral, like a good son should. And thanks to making amends to him, I was "square" with him and could say good-bye without any regrets.

Three years later, when my mom got sick, I was there for her too. The result of that was that she decided she didn't have to live alone. Finally, she consented to me building a wing for her on the back of my house and getting her out of the old neighborhood. I don't have the right to rob her of her independence to satisfy my need to know she is taken care of. Her apartment is totally self-contained, except for the laundry room, which we share. Mom has her own entry to a garden area and flowerbed, so she can do the gardening she loves so much. Her place has many windows, so she can have plenty of light to paint.

Some folks use the term making "living amends" when you can't have one of those frank and honest talks. But really, isn't changing the way we do things the true spirit of making direct amends? I'll never be able to undo my past, but I don't have to continue to be haunted by it if I just follow the path that has been laid out for me by those who trudged the road before me.

Don A.
Germantown, Tennessee

The Dad I Could Love
March 2013

I was seven years sober and heading back to my home state when I was encouraged by a longtime member and close friend to look up my father. My dad and I have had a less than good relationship. For the past 30 years, we have only seen or spoken with each other a dozen or so times.

My friend knew I had to face these difficulties surrounding my father. So in the summer of 2000, I drove 200 miles away, without a phone number or address, and pulled into Bozeman, Montana. I looked in the phone book, found my father's name and called him. He answered. When I said, "Hello," he promptly replied, "What do you want?" I expressed my need to speak with him and assured him it wouldn't take long.

Within 15 minutes, I found myself on my dad's front porch. As I tried to clean my side of the street, he said some very nasty, ugly things to me. I finished my amend and was back on the road within a half hour. While driving away from his house I felt extremely proud of myself, because I did not get caught up in the same old behavior. It was not until later that I realized it wasn't that I was proud, it was that I had been humbled by the program.

Four years later, I was standing at work on a loading dock when my phone rang. I answered, and much to my surprise, I heard a voice saying, "Happy birthday, son." I talked with my father for about 20 minutes.

Later that same evening, I shared this experience with my daughter. She told me she would like to meet him. Five months later, we were visiting my dad and his wife for the first time in 15 years. My daughter and I now travel to Montana every summer to visit him, and I speak with him quite often.

Because of the actions I have taken in Alcoholics Anonymous, the father I despised has become the dad I could love.

Smoochie
Tacoma, Washington

I Get to Be With Her
September 2015

S he sits there, allowing me to hold her hand. Not really sure who I am, my mother nevertheless seems to find comfort in my presence. How difficult it was for her when she was in that twilight that comes with early-stage dementia, knowing that her mind was slipping away, that she should know people she didn't, especially her own son and daughter. But now that time has passed, a small blessing I suppose, so that she's content to not know as long as things don't get too confusing to her, so that she becomes agitated.

And that has become my job, to see to it that my mother, the woman who brought me into this world, is not overly stressed out with life. Being retired, I get to spend about 40 hours a week with her, while my sister and her husband are at work helping others. Mom lives with them now, and I'm so grateful there can always be someone with her if she calls out in the middle of the night. My daughter also helps from time to time when I need to get away. So we're holding it together with God's help.

I am glad to be here for my mother, something I could not do 19 years ago. I simply couldn't make time to show up for life. I missed so much of my children's growing up and other family activities, because even when I was present, I wasn't there. The twilights I experienced in my own life were the result of being too stupefied with booze to speak, wanting to join in the conversations around me but knowing I would only slur my words and get those disapproving looks from whichever wife I was married to at the time. But no more ...

not since April 30, 1995. I began a journey in the Fellowship of AA.

Now I get to be with my mother when she needs me the most. I am where I am supposed to be, doing what I am supposed to be doing. I get to take her out to eat at her favorite restaurant, where a friend always serves us and prepares for our coming. Even when there's a waiting line, she manages to find a way in for us so that my mother doesn't have to wait. Once after we had eaten but were still sitting there, my mother reached across the table to squeeze my hand and said, "I missed you so much!" Though she was looking at me, I could tell she was speaking to my father, who's been dead 16 years. I squeezed her hand back and replied, "I missed you too."

I sit once again with her hand in mine and she is at peace. I've been granted the opportunity to be here now with my mother. And as I hold her hand at this moment, I realize she too is holding mine.

Ed M.
Louisville, Kentucky

Making Amends
(From Dear Grapevine)
January 1990

The September article on the Ninth Step, entitled "Fear Gave Way to Faith," prompts my letter. In this article John H. recalls his anguish at being unable to make amends to his mother because she died before he gained sobriety.

As the mother of a recovering alcoholic, I speculated on what I would have missed not knowing of my son's new happiness. Certainly I would have missed my anxiety, fear and pain turned to joy, but mostly I would have regretted not being able to tell him, "You do make amends to me each time you reach out to a newcomer."

C. M.
Harrison, Ohio

What I Do *Owe*
September 2016

My father was an alcoholic, but for years, in my mind I still wasn't as bad as he was. He lived on the Bowery, sleeping in unlocked cars, on fleabag pallets in mission houses and, when all else failed, wrapped in a cardboard box in an alley somewhere. He never supported my mother and her four children. On the rare occasions when we saw him, he stole precious coins from Mom's purse and beat us all up if we complained.

I had resentments. "What did he ever do for me?" I demanded of my sponsor when he said I might owe my father an amends. I was a drunk too, but somehow I managed to support my family. I couldn't hold onto a job, but I was good at getting new ones. We had to move 13 times in the first 15 years of our marriage. A pre-employment doctor giving me a physical exam told me I was getting gouty, but I swore to him that I didn't drink, so he said, "Don't eat any more Brussels sprouts or lima beans." I gave them both up and then lost that job, then another, and finally bought a pistol, seeing a .38 slug as the only reasonable solution left.

"What did he ever do for me?" I whined. "He never gave me anything. He never cared."

My sponsor saw it differently. "How did you get to AA? How did you know where to go for help?" he asked me.

"My father was in and out of AA all of his adult life," I told him. "He never made it work for him. He died on skid row."

When I left my sponsor after this discussion in a church basement, I went home and brooded. I liked brooding. Feeling sorry for myself seemed to justify all the anger I carried, all the guilt for my own bad behavior, and the thoughts of what might have been. Self-indulgence, self-pity and a whisky on the rocks had carried me for years, but what does one do sober?

I live in Eastern Pennsylvania. My father was buried in Minnesota in a small churchyard near the old family farm. I didn't like listening to my sponsor, but I decided to consider what he had said about getting right with my father. I drove all the way out there only to learn that he was in an unmarked grave. It took some effort to find the church sexton, who looked in the record book and then showed me to the right spot. I stood at my father's grave. I stood and stood—clueless.

After a while, it occurred to me that I didn't owe him an amends after all. I had never done anything to hurt him, never said anything mean and in fact, had rarely ever seen him. But I realized that I did owe him understanding. He was an alcoholic, and so was I. That I hadn't fallen as low as he had was due more to the circumstances of my mother's influence on my education and training than to anything else. I simply began life at a higher base point. My mother was a rare gem.

I owed my father forgiveness as well as understanding. Though he was a hopeless drunk, I couldn't take his inventory. I had no idea what went on in his life. It had to have been horrible. I had to accept that that's who he was—a man without a prayer, alone. It could well have been me except for circumstances and some good people in Alcoholics Anonymous.

I left the gravesite and went to a place that sold monuments and bought my father a headstone to mark his grave. On my way home, I couldn't help thinking about the pistol I had bought. I was grateful that on that fateful night I had drunk myself into a blackout and forgot what my purpose had been. I was still alive. Hope and love filled my life. My sons had accepted me back to the land of the living. My wife, whose patience is beyond imagination, is still my wife.

"Does God love me?" I ask. Lord knows, somebody does. I sure didn't get here with 33 years of sobriety by myself.

Leon A.
Doylestown, Pennsylvania

Under the Banyan Tree
August 2013

When I wrote my first Eighth Step list, I had no trouble putting my mother at the top. In my Fourth Step, I had already itemized what I had stolen from her (money, jewelry, wedding silver). I knew what came next.

Admitting guilt has always been difficult for me. Lying came easily. I think my mother's legendary temper played a part in this. I grew up with her raging over even minor infractions. Frequently, as she said herself, she would completely come unglued. I felt that I needed to evade guilt at all costs. I had no doubt, after telling her the truth, that she would come completely unglued.

I put her name on the list, though not out of courage. I knew that I would never have to admit anything to her. She died before I got sober.

I expected my sponsor to say to move on, but he didn't. Instead, he told me how alcoholics have been making amends to dead parents since the very beginning of AA.

He had me write a letter to my mother, being very specific about what I had stolen. I gave it to him to read over. He asked me to take out the references to my mother's temper and to rewrite the letter on something nicer than cheap notebook paper. He told me to seal it in an envelope and mail it. It seemed absurd to use a stamp, since the envelope was addressed to "Mom," but he said to do it anyway.

The next week, we met at a diner to talk about what came next: forgiveness.

I didn't think my mother was any more likely to forgive me dead than alive. He wasn't talking about her forgiving me, however, but me forgiving her. I didn't think this was something I could do. He said that I had only begun to make my amends. He suggested that I go back to my hometown to leave flowers at my mother's grave. I made the trip, knowing that she had not been buried beside her parents. Her brother had not allowed it. Seeing her surrounded by strangers made me feel sorry for her, something new.

Next, I contacted my mother's beloved aunt, who had always given my mother love and encouragement. My mother frequently mentioned how grateful she was. My aunt burst into tears. She had felt guilty that she hadn't done enough. She then told me stories about my mother as a little girl, who sounded nothing like the woman I knew. She sent me a small album of fading photos of my parents' wedding. I hadn't realized how much my mother once looked like a young Katherine Hepburn. In one photo, she is flashing a dazzling, confident smile. I clearly didn't know this young woman.

I got back into contact with my siblings. I had virtually no relationship with either of them. I had moved away when they were barely out of grade school. I now attempted to be their older brother, something my mother would have wanted. To my surprise, my siblings responded. I ended up doing for them what my mother's aunt had done for me—fill in gaps in the past.

I was in the seventh grade when my parents divorced. My father moved away and remarried. My mother had to go to work to support us. In 1970, her options were very limited. We went on food stamps. She lost whatever control over her drinking that she once had. She went out every night and frequently did not come home at all. I would wake up some mornings to find strange men in the house. I think my moving away after high school scared her. She quickly remarried. She still drank heavily, but now at home. My siblings grew up with an angry stepfather, but it wasn't the reign of terror that I had known.

My siblings often didn't recognize the mother I described. I couldn't chalk this up simply to the gap in age between us. Their impressions frequently differed from each other. This opened my eyes to a particular kind of self-centeredness. Other people didn't necessarily experience the world as I did. I also realized that I had to make an amend to them.

On the night my mother died, I rushed back to her house and went directly to the basement, hoping to save old family photos from an inevitable purge. I found a box stuffed with scrapbooks and albums. I put it in the trunk of my car. I didn't tell my stepfather or my siblings what I had done. Old habits die hard, especially with "noble" motives.

I also told my siblings that I grew up feeling that our mother didn't care about me. They asked if this was why I vanished from their lives after high school. In those years, I kept contact with my mother to a minimum. I wouldn't answer her calls or return her messages. This went on for years. I now understand that I was inflicting a new kind of harm, what a wise member of my home group calls "causing suspicion." This is when a child's neglect makes a parent wonder if something bad has happened. I caused my mother to worry all the time. Had there been an accident? Was I in the hospital? Was I even alive? How do I know that she worried about me? In my third year, I finally opened the box that I had taken. My mother kept a journal of sorts. She wrote down just how much she had worried about me.

I had one especially resilient resentment against my mother. On days when she drank at home, she liked to crank up her Hawaiian records and dance the hula for the neighbors. I felt humiliated and was teased relentlessly. My sponsor and I talked about this. I mentioned that my mother had lived briefly in Hawaii as a teenager. She considered this to be one of the happiest periods of her life. She loved Hawaiian culture and became an accomplished hula dancer. Before my parents married, she set up a small hula school in our hometown, one of the first of its kind on the mainland. I heard these stories directly from her, usually when her drinking turned weepy. I went to the hotel where my parents honeymooned and sat outside, nursing a pineapple juice. I realized that I had acquired my mother's love of Hawaii, the first place where I finally felt somewhat comfortable in my skin. I wondered if it did something similar for her. After all this, I wish I could say that I had finally forgiven my mother.

In year seven, I started experiencing can't-get-out-of-bed depression. I turned to therapy, and my mother kept coming up over and over. My therapist seemed impressed by my amends. I didn't understand why. It had accomplished nothing. I continued to go to meetings and have service commitments, but nothing seemed to bring any relief. I told myself not to drink, no matter what, but I had no hope that anything would ever change.

Then, one day, everything changed. I made another trip to Hawaii, this time to attend an AA convention. One night, I went back to the hotel where my parents had honeymooned. The hotel is built around an enormous old banyan tree with a dense canopy of leafy branches. I ordered my pineapple juice. The waves crashed on the beach. A man played the ukulele. An old woman, her cloud of silver hair sitting on her shoulders like a shawl, sang Hawaiian songs that seemed familiar; they were ones my mother used to sing. I heard a burst of laughter from behind me. I watched a waitress take a picture of a young couple seated at a nearby table. I heard the young man, already bald, say that they were on their honeymoon. His beautiful bride had an enormous yellow hibiscus flower in her hair.

A memory hit me upside the head. I already had the photo the waitress just snapped, only it was faded and black-and-white. I came across it in that box that I had swiped from my mother's basement. In that old photo, there's a banyan tree, probably this one. My parents are the happy couple on their honeymoon. My father is already bald, and my mother has a big flower in her hair. They look so happy. Their future must have looked so bright to her. She could not have imagined what alcoholism would do to her dreams, her marriage, her children.

I suddenly felt overwhelmed by compassion for her. She was just like other women sitting around me in AA meetings, the ones who had loved and helped me countless times. The only difference was this: she had not gotten the gift of sobriety. All the anger and resentment vanished then and there. That was more than 10 years ago and it has not come back.

I don't sugarcoat my childhood. My mother may have done the best she could, but she did a lousy job. Still, I forgive her everything. It took finding compassion for her to do that. When I wrote that first letter, I had no idea how many years and different ways this amend would take. Fortunately, I kept trying, even though my efforts seemed to fail. Now, I think my "failures" actually prepared me for that moment under the banyan tree for the spiritual awakening about my mother.

Anonymous

CHAPTER THREE

Offering Our Amends to the Children We Love

———◇———

Tender or tough, Step Nine offers both parents and children a new birth day

" I got my list out. At the top were two daughters and two sons." One son Corinne H. hadn't seen in 15 years, the other two children not for seven years, she writes in this chapter's story "The Mending Process." This will be a process indeed, since one of them will not listen to her amends. "But this I know for sure—when my Higher Power thinks my son and I are ready for each other, we will be reunited." Though Ronny H. was "a happy-go-lucky" drunk who thought he didn't need Steps Eight and Nine, in the story "A New Itinerary," he happily babysits his grandchildren as a living amends "for years of wasted days and wasted nights."

Our relationships with our children are often complicated enough without the need for healing that follows alcoholic child-rearing. But it's then that Step Nine can be a miracle of reconciliation. "Not unlike most children of alcoholic parents," writes Colleen C. in "I Know Where You See God," "my little boy was emotionally abandoned," troubled by a drunken mother behind the wheel. In the story "My Superhero," Tom W.'s initial promises to his neglected daughters were "met with that uncomfortable Step Nine silence," but he persisted and becomes a hero in his daughter's yes.

And in the article "Amends," Jeanne W., a sober grandma who's making living amends by helping raise the children of the daughter she once threw out, happily puts it right out there: "Grandmothers should not be drunk."

The Mending Process
September 1993

D uring my first month in Alcoholics Anonymous I did what so many have done before me—I decided, without benefit of sponsor or sanity, to immediately make amends. For years I had been attending church every time the doors opened, hoping something would help me (it never occurred to me to quit drinking). In my prayer group was a woman who irritated the bejabbers out of me. How I tried to help that woman learn to pray! I behaved very badly. Upon my getting dry she was the very first person I decided to make amends to. I called and said something like, "Dora, I just wanted to tell you that I love you," and she promptly replied, "Thanks one whole heckuva lot," and hung up on me. I was crushed!

Each of the Twelve Steps has required, for me, a new surrender. And Step Nine was no different. For a long time I agonized because nothing seemed to be happening as I wandered through Steps Eight and Nine. There was no comfort, no sense of having "taken" Step Nine. I walked around for a time saying, "I'm sorry." But that didn't feel right. That had been one of my favorite responses after every drunk and overdose. Those who had heard it over and over during those awful years were more than a little skeptical of this repeat phrase. Finally it seemed to me the only choice I had was one more surrender, one more throwing in the towel. I can't, he can, we will.

I never surrender gracefully. After being told by one of those quiet, serene old-timers to pray for willingness, I went home, stormed, ranted and raved, and generally behaved like five years old instead of 50. Finally, a sponsor's admonition to "read the Big Book" dawned. I read. I cried. I finally fell to my knees and said to old HP, "You already know my needs and wants, so from now on I'll do my best—just please help me." No more bargains, threats, or drunken pleas. Another surrender!

I got my list out. At the top were two daughters and two sons. One daughter I had already started making amends to by being sober, caring and responsible. I could see her acceptance of me. The three other children were another matter. One son I hadn't seen in 15 years, the other two not for seven years. How to make the approach?

The day after my ranting and raving, I awoke to a hot August morning with a great sense of peace—yet a feeling that the day would bring something. At eleven o'clock my phone rang. My daughter's voice on the other end was saying, "Mom. I'm going to have a baby. Can I write to you?" She lived 700 miles away. She told me her youngest brother was in the Navy, and her oldest brother was married and expecting his first child.

And so it began. The God of my understanding gave me the opportunity to begin the mending process. What a lot of hill climbing that has been. And as with most hills, sometimes it's up and at times it's straight down. Then there are the plateaus, when it seems like I'm just marking time.

The pregnant daughter and youngest son are now "home again." The oldest son—that's another matter. I wrote him a letter trying to tell him how sorry I was that I left him when he was 12 years old. Two years after the first attempt, he allowed me to see his wife and son, but wouldn't see me himself. Sometime later he developed Hodgkin's disease. Through the years, I'm told, he also developed alcoholism. As far as I know, he has chosen not to treat either of his diseases. He still will not accept my amends, 15 years after my first attempts. There are so many times I wish God's timetable was the same as mine. But this I know for sure—when my Higher Power thinks my son and I are ready for each other, we will be reunited. I have undying faith. It has happened before. It will happen again.

The great revelation for me was that direct amends are not a thinking or wishing process. Direct amends are action-oriented. Words are necessary for people to hear that I am trying to mend my ways, but it is the living out of the principles of this program that counts.

Corinne H.
Raleigh, North Carolina

A New Itinerary
(From Dear Grapevine)
October 2003

I sobered up in September 1988, but Steps Eight and Nine were not on my itinerary for many years. I was a "happy-go-lucky" drunk most of the time. My misery surfaced only after I tried to control my drinking. I did apologize to my wife every time I came out of detox, though. In Madras, India, detox was expensive. The money spent on detox for three days could have kept me gloriously drunk for one month. I felt this was the only thing that hurt my wife. The money I spent on myself could have been put to better use.

Now, I am a landed immigrant in Canada. I came here to babysit my grandchildren. I took this job to make amends for years of wasted days and wasted nights that I did not spend with my own children. I do this to the best of my ability. It leaves me drained at the end of the day. The feeling is good, though. I am making myself useful to members of my family.

I came to Alcoholics Anonymous with a problem. I found God in Alcoholics Anonymous with a solution. I have hope, and hope is the feeling I have that "the feeling I have" will get better.

Ronny H.
Scarborough, Ontario

My Superhero
September 2015

"**D**ad, are you going to stop drinking for a little while, or are you going to stop forever?" I wasn't prepared for my 7-year-old daughter's question. I paused for a moment. I really didn't know how to answer her. So I said, "Forever, if I can, Shanny."

She smiled and cheered like a cheerleader, "You can do it! You can do it! Forever! Forever!"

At the time, I wasn't sure I could stay sober for even the next 24 hours, but her question put me on the hook. I didn't want to let her down again. Not now.

When I first attended AA, I was a divorced father living apart from my kids. AA gave me hope for the first time that I could stay sober. As I worked through my Fourth and Fifth Steps with my sponsor, I realized I was not the "World's Greatest Dad," as stated on the little statuette I received as a Father's Day present. I hadn't spent time with my two girls in my drinking years. I was busy trying to find a replacement for their mom. Even when I was with them, I wasn't really present.

The weekend before, I had admitted to the girls that I hadn't been the father I should have been. I told them I was going to be the best dad I could be now. This statement was met with that uncomfortable Step Nine silence. The scariest part was saying, "I love you," to my daughters. I had never told them this before. Shanny smiled wide and gave me a big hug. She said, "I know Dad, and I love you, too!" My oldest daughter, Sarah, turned away without a word. This would have devastated me if I hadn't noticed the slow trickle of a tear on her cheek. I felt like I had broken through her armor to touch her heart, which she kept hidden from me.

Shanny didn't waste any time taking me up on my offer. She asked me to attend her baseball games, and I agreed, though I worried her games would interfere with my AA meetings. Then she added the up-coming parent-teacher conference to her growing list.

The conference was scheduled for the same night as my home group, so I could have gotten out of it. I really did not want to set foot in that school. I worried I wouldn't know what to say to a teacher. But I had given Shanny my "better father" speech, and I remembered what my sponsor often said: "Act your way into better thinking." I knew I had to go.

The night of the conference, I drove by the old house we used to live in, which brought back memories. The old gingko tree near the side-walk still stood where the girls learned to ride their bikes. I remembered being passed out on the cold bathroom floor when I was supposed to be watching Shanny. I didn't wake up until I heard my wife calling me. Opening my eyes, I saw my little girl holding a towel like Linus from Peanuts, staring at my drunken carcass curled around the toilet. My wife never said a word. There would be many more of these nights.

I drove on, and as I approached my kids' home I saw Shanny stand-ing in the door waiting. She yelled, "Right on time, Dad!"

I hadn't been on time for years of Fridays, picking up the girls for weekend custody. Back then I would head to the hotel bar and slam as many beers as I could after work. I was always late to pick them up. As soon as I opened the door, Shanny would run to me full speed and jump into my arms, announcing, "Daddy, you smell like bee-ow again!" Her speech impediment stretched beer into a two-syllable word. I always put my finger to her lips to quiet her before her mother heard. I know now I wasn't fooling anyone.

I parked the car at the school. Shanny jumped out and said, "I can't wait for you to meet my teachers." She pulled me along by the hand. I was stepping out of my old life into a new world of fatherhood. I felt my gut tighten. I didn't know what to expect of these strangers, these "normies," as I liked to call them. I wanted to get this over fast.

Shanny rushed to the entrance and opened the door. As I stepped in, the familiar smell of old textbooks caught me and made me feel a bit more comfortable. Shanny and I had made a habit of stopping in to bookstores. We both loved the smell of books. It was something we shared.

"Come on, Dad," Shanny said. "Let me take you to my first class of the day."

Her English teacher sat at an old oak desk. I didn't make eye contact with her at first because I was distracted by watching Shanny digging into a box in the corner of the room. Her teacher was young and professionally dressed. I looked at my faded blue jeans and scuffed leather boots. I felt very out of place.

Just then Shanny returned from the corner of the room and slapped me on my chest. She said, "My daddy stopped drinking bee-ow!" Looking down at my shirt, I found a sticker that said, "Drug Free" in big red letters. Shanny had the biggest grin on her face.

I didn't know what to say. But I noticed her teacher was grinning, too. I realized Shanny must have shared my story with her. I sheepishly smiled.

The English teacher was a good sport. She didn't say a word, and instead pulled out Shanny's progress report. "I don't know if you realize it," she said, "but Shannon is reading at the fifth- and sixth-grade level. This is quite rare and extraordinary for a second-grade student."

"That's great!" I said. I looked at Shanny, and in that moment I felt a real connection. I realized those trips we made to the bookstore meant a lot to Shanny, and to me.

Shanny then took my hand and escorted me through her other classrooms. Soon I found it easier to make small talk with the teachers. Especially after that first one! Her progress reports were glowing, which made me so proud and happy for her. We both were beaming!

"There is one more classroom I want to take you to, Dad." This time she did not take my hand. She shook her hands back and forth, which was something she did when she felt nervous.

I followed her into the room. She said, "I want to show you my project." She pointed at what looked like hundreds of sheets of paper stapled to a huge wall. They looked like a giant quilt, each with its own colored artwork. I stepped closer and saw drawings of Superman, Batman and Spiderman saving helpless victims with sad faces.

"Here's mine, Dad. I hope you like it." She stood in front of her project, pointing it out and looking up at me with hopeful eyes.

On the wall was a picture of a man with long hair and black boots. The title was "My Superhero Is My Dad." I melted. Tears ran down my face. I tried to wipe them away, but it was no use, they just kept coming. In that moment, I realized I wasn't a screwup. I had a chance to make it better. I was her father and I felt an overwhelming forgiveness, acceptance and love. In this moment, I became unafraid for the first time and stepped through that door to a whole new world that opened up. My little girl needed me. She loved me in spite of my drinking and my demons. I was transformed that day. I felt worthy of being a father.

"Do you like you my project?" she asked.

"Yes, yes Shanny, I do." I could barely get the words out. Wiping tears away, I saw that her project included notes about my sobriety in AA and my recent service work at the Red Cross. She had drawn the two of us together, holding hands and smiling.

The picture healed me as a father forever. I woke up and was enlightened by a daughter who needed me as I needed her love to heal the scars I carried from my past. No matter how unworthy I felt of her love, there she was standing in front of me with her little arms wide open.

Tom W.
West Des Moines, Iowa

I Know Where You See God
(From Dear Grapevine)
May 1997

One of the greatest gifts I have received in sobriety is, without a doubt, my relationship with my little boy. Not unlike most children of alcoholic parents, he was emotionally abandoned and left to do his growing up on his own. It was a pretty tough road for a kid who wasn't yet eight years old. He watched, sad and confused, as his mom sat on the couch pouring booze down her throat. I was one of those "good mothers" who drank at home.

By the time I got to Alcoholics Anonymous, I was in the depths of despair, afraid to quit drinking, and terrified if I didn't quit I was going to die. The guilt I was facing as a mom was unbelievable; the shame, insurmountable. I was told that if I had faith in a power greater than myself, good things would begin to happen. Having nothing else to lose, I grabbed onto that idea, and slowly my life did begin to change. I went to lots of meetings, tried to keep an open mind, and did what was suggested. I was blessed with a sponsor who got me involved in service work, and I discovered fun. Before I knew it, I had some real friends and real love.

Instead of leaving my son at home, I took him to meetings with me, not always, but enough that he could be a part of his mom's new way of life. I didn't know if, at the age of eight, he'd be able to grasp any of what was going on, but still feeling those guilt pangs, I didn't want to leave him behind anymore.

Soon, I was able to work my way through the Steps and begin to make some amends. As I made my amends to him, he was able to tell me how he'd felt during my drinking days. He told me I'd ignored him a lot and wasn't honest with him. He was also angry that I'd driven our car while drinking, with him in it. Had I not taken the Steps suggested in this program I'd never have been able to live with those few statements my little boy shared with me.

My Higher Power has been with me from the start, guiding me on this path. When things are going a little rough, I go to a meeting. When things are going really good, I still go to a meeting. I know if I'm to stay spiritually charged, I need to be continuously plugged into the rooms of AA. And if I have any doubts about whether there's a God of my understanding in those rooms, all I have to do is ask my son.

One day while we were discussing things we believe in but can't see, he said, "Mom, I know where you see God—in your meetings."

Colleen C.
Lake Stevens, Washington

The Luckiest Mom
February 2006

One of the promises in the Big Book talks about not regretting the past, nor shutting the door on it. My past was filled with shame, degradation, and terrible losses because of my alcoholism. But when a loving sponsor guided me through the Steps, I experienced both divine and human forgiveness.

The greatest pain that resulted from my alcoholism came from losing my baby daughter. I made a decision to give her up for adoption before she was born. In 1971, my drinking was out of control prior to my pregnancy. The only reason I didn't drink while pregnant was because alcohol made me sick.

I went through the nine months dry and filled with self-hatred, shame, depression and terrible guilt. I used an adoption agency that, in those days, offered no counseling to me. Every day I woke up with a sense of total uncertainty. I did not feel capable of raising a child by myself, and deep down I didn't feel as though I deserved a child because I was so very bad. When she was born, I held her briefly before she left for her new world. A piece of my soul died when they took her away.

For the next eight years, I tried to drink myself to death, tried to block out the misery and pain I felt. Although I was always unsuccessful at suicide, alcoholism is a very slow suicide. I was unable to maintain relationships, jobs, dreams, plans, and eventually, unable to maintain anything.

My disease progressed quickly and I became totally immersed in a vodka bottle. My family offered me money to get rid of me. I was arrested; my friends sat on bar stools in dark, seedy places; and I whirled through the lives of many innocent people, leaving wreckage wherever I went.

I became hopeless. I thought about my daughter whenever I saw a child. I worried about her safety and wallowed in self-pity over my decision to give her up. I was a drunken martyr and not a pretty sight. It seemed that I had lost everything important.

It is only by God's grace that I am sober today, and I am grateful to be a member of Alcoholics Anonymous. In AA, I found the opportunity to face the truth in every area of my life.

When I came into the program, I knew in my heart that I was finally home. I felt safe for the first time in my life. I desperately wanted to stay sober and was willing to do whatever I was told. However, being an egomaniac with no self-worth, I balked at doing an inventory. Finally, the day came. I was either going to drink, or I was going to write a Fourth Step and share it with my sponsor.

My biggest secret was the loss of my daughter. I finally got everything out, but the wound took years to heal. I thought I had forgiven myself many times, but the shame and guilt seemed to linger. I felt an empty place in my heart that nothing could fill. Today, I realize that God fills the holes in my heart if only I seek him. My biggest problem was resolving the conflict within myself. I could not understand how anyone, including me, would give up a child. My husband and I never had children because I did not think I deserved to have another baby. My selfishness was costly to a lot of people.

One night I was sitting in a meeting on the Eighth Step, when someone said they continued to add to their amends list over time in an attempt to become more honest in their recovery. I immediately thought of my daughter and how I had not known how to make amends, since I had no idea where she was.

The action I took was to call the adoption agency and ask to place information about myself on file. I did not want to search for her, but I wanted her to be able to know who I was if she ever decided to look for me. They sent me a legal form to complete that I held for several years. My fear that she would hate me was very great for a long time.

In 1992, I filled out the form, wrote a letter to my daughter about myself and enclosed some photographs. I got on my knees and asked

God only for his will to be done. I felt a sense of freedom because this was my attempt at amends. I went on with my life and recovery. On her birthday, I usually wrote to my precious child in my journal. I knew that God was totally in charge of the outcome. Each time I talked about my daughter I felt a bit lighter. I remember leading an Eighth Step meeting and talking about the loss. Several other people in the meeting shared about losing their children because of alcoholism. I was not alone anymore.

In 1994, I received a telephone call from the adoption agency. "Pat, this is a wonderful day," the woman said. "Your daughter wants to talk with you, and she wants to meet you."

We set up a call time for that very night; I cried for the rest of the day. My AA sponsor and my sponsor from another program came to my apartment to support me. I prayed for guidance and strength.

The phone rang and I heard her voice, which sounded a lot like my own. I answered her questions and we began a relationship that is absolutely awesome. She sent pictures of herself, and our resemblance is remarkable. I flew to the city where she lives to meet her.

I spent that weekend in the middle of Step Nine. I did not excuse my behavior, I did not blame my alcoholism, and I knew that I had to be very honest with her. We talked for hours and hours and we both cried a lot. She is a beautiful woman with a forgiving heart and soul. Her family had always told her she was a gift, and that I loved her very much.

My perception of her feelings was completely wrong. She had never felt anything except love and curiosity about me. Her adoptive mother and I have a wonderful relationship and have spent time together. She did a beautiful job raising my daughter, and I owe her a huge debt of gratitude. Everyone in my daughter's family has welcomed me with unconditional love.

Since our first meeting was about getting the truth out, our relationship has not been mired with excess baggage. We have a very special bond as friends who respect, honor and love the women we have become. I attended her college graduation and her wedding. We talk on the phone often, and she really enjoys coming to visit me.

She has often commented about the quality of my relationship with women in AA. Ironically, she came into my life at a time when I have less materially in recovery than I have ever had. I know that God wants me to just be me, without any trimmings. I have been available to her on a deep emotional level, and have not tried to control one aspect of this relationship, which is a miracle. In my heart of hearts, I understand that this is another precious gift from God, and that is how I treat her. The hole in my heart is filled and overflows with love today.

None of this would have been possible without the other gift in my life: sobriety and the program of Alcoholics Anonymous. I feel divine forgiveness and sometimes believe I'm the luckiest mom in the world. Recently, I got a card from her that said: "I am so lucky because I have two wonderful mothers."

Pat T.
Houston, Texas

Amends
(From Dear Grapevine)
September 1994

My husband and I raised six children. During that time my drinking got progressively worse, and by the time they reached the teenage years I was a drunk, depressed, crying mess.

Somewhere during those years my daughter and I began a real dislike of each other. We had a running verbal battle for years until finally, in a drunken rage, I threw her out.

Quite a few years have passed since then. I got sober nine years ago and she married and became the mother of three. About five years ago I made my amends to her. She told me I just wanted to get myself off the hook and that I wasn't really sorry. We had a cool but ongoing relationship after that.

As I moved along in sobriety, I learned I could not change others, only work on myself. I did—and I got healthier and healthier.

Today, my daughter has a husband who has left his family to drink and drug. She has been forced to raise her children alone. It is my greatest blessing to help her raise my grandchildren. I can be there for them when they need a grandmother and for my daughter when she needs a mother.

All our past problems are just that. Past and forgiven. We are friends now. I am so grateful to the program for showing me the way of forgiveness, perseverance and prayer.

I'm so happy to be sober and free. Grandmothers should not be drunk.

Jeanne W.
Lynn, Massachusetts

Leaving the Results to God
March 1999

My name is Mary and I'm an alcoholic and the mother of two sons. My sons were raised in a sick, alcoholic home. I am the mother whose drinking progressed into rage and madness. I am the mother who verbally abused and physically beat my little boys. I could not stop myself from my own actions. I knew I was wrong and I could not stop. King Alcohol owned me body and soul.

I ran away from my home on the East Coast when my sons were in their late teens. I tried to start over but I brought my bottle with me. Finally, after a few attempts, I began my sobriety in September 1979.

After a couple of months I asked a lady to be my sponsor. She had dignity in her life. I wanted that for myself. She got me going on the Steps right away. I was so ashamed of my life and of what I had become. When I said to her, "What shall I do?" her answer was, "Do the Steps. Start with Step One." She and I went to Step meetings together and read the Steps together at her kitchen table. We talked, wrote and laughed. Thank God for her humor. She gave me hope, and I was willing to learn.

Eventually I got to Step Nine. I was so afraid I'd do it wrong but God prepared the way for me. My firstborn was now in his early 20's and was visiting from his home on the East Coast. We were alone together in a peaceful, beautiful place, and I began saying my amends. He let me talk and was completely accepting of my words. It was one of the most frightening and courageous times of my life, and one of the most rewarding. Our relationship is healing and our love for each other is better and better as time goes on.

I wish this had been the case with my younger son. When I approached him in order to make my amends, he stopped me and said he didn't want to hear my "stuff." He said he didn't believe I was alcoholic and that I was using this as an excuse. God gave me the courage to sit still and listen to him. When he was finished I was able to tell him that I loved him very much and that it didn't matter if he believed I was alcoholic. The fact that I believe I am is what's important. This took place in my first year of sobriety, and we have not had such a talk again (I've been sober for 18 years). Our relationship has a long way to go today.

I have done a lot of Step work—inventories, Fifth Steps with my sponsors, praying and releasing my son to God. Our program has given me the courage and dignity to go on with my life and see my value as a sober woman. I have shared my experience with many AA young men and women, some of whom have been very close to my son's age and who grew up with a drunken mom like me.

AA has taught me that our Higher Power is our source for all that is good for us and for others. As I trust this wonderful program, I leave the results to God and I go about doing what I am supposed to do: stay sober, go to meetings, live the Steps and say yes to AA's principles and Traditions. I don't know if my younger son and I will heal our relationship. I have to continue to be willing to do my part. The rest is up to God's wisdom.

Mary P.
Morro Bay, California

CHAPTER FOUR

Bringing Our Amends Back Home

◇

When our addiction has rippled through our family,
healing can too

The statement, "It's a family disease," a familiar reminder at our AA meetings, is brought to life on the pages in this section. Jamie C., in "The Fire Has Gone Out," sees mutual damages everywhere as he looks at his aunts, uncles, cousins and grandparents. In the story "Made Direct Amends," R.B. writes, "In taking Step Nine ... I was walking across a bridge that had already been built by my Higher Power, time and sobriety." Also titled "Made Direct Amends," Carol S.'s story tells how she married into a family of grudge-holders and "drank the alcoholic's bitter brew of anger, resentments and bewildering despair," till she spoke her amends with humility and dignity, stunning her family into peace. "Making amends started a chain reaction of forgiveness that changed a whole family," writes Carol, adding that she "learned more from the amends I swore I'd never make than from any other person or event in my recovery."

An amends made to a family is the deepest and truest of family reunions.

The Fire Has Gone Out
September 1997

I didn't have to be told that in the years of my drinking I damaged those closest to me. My wife's tears and the pain on my children's faces as I erupted again and again in alcoholic rage played a large part in bringing me to crisis and then into recovery. I knew I needed to make amends to them. I wanted to put my involvement with my family on a healthy, functioning and mutually-rewarding basis. There was work to be done, and lots of it.

The Big Book turned out to be right: my wife and children were generous in accepting my apologies, eager to help me heal, happy that the long nightmare in which we all had lived was now over. But that was only the beginning of the process of making amends to them. My apologies, no matter how sincere, were not enough. I'd damaged my loved ones and deprived them of the kind of husband and father they had a right to expect. Now I needed to grow out of self-centeredness and selfishness, and to learn to look at the world from their point of view in order to understand what I might do for them. I had to find new ways of communicating with them. All of this took time, to say nothing of that rare quality, patience! It wasn't by accident, I realized, that we undertake the Ninth Step only after we ourselves have become strong enough to embark on the kind of spiritual work that amends-making requires. Perhaps we can expect the Promises to come true only after we've started making amends within the family.

As difficult as this process sometimes was in relation to my wife and children, it took on a new dimension when I turned to making amends within my family of origin. In my own immediate family, the major damages were done by me, and I was the one who needed forgiveness. But there had been no knights in shining armor in my family of origin. My alcoholic father damaged my codependent mother and she damaged him; frightened and angry as I was, I damaged both of them and they damaged me. Aunts and uncles and cousins and grandparents—mutual damages seemed to be everywhere. Everyone was a player, and in all honesty—perhaps because I'd left home in my mid-teens—my contribution to those damages had been relatively small.

But I still needed to clean my side of the street, and I saw that I had to begin by forgiving those who had hurt me. With smoldering resentments still eating at me, I couldn't be really effective in making amends. I hadn't expected it, but forgiving others for the injury they had done to me was a necessary part of my Ninth Step.

But what would it mean for me to forgive those relatives of mine who had made my childhood so unhappy? Clearly it was more than merely mouthing the words, "I forgive you." But what more? And how was it to be done? The Big Book, so helpful in many other matters, didn't really give me the direction I needed. Neither did the "Twelve and Twelve." In a small handful of places, both sources mentioned the necessity of forgiveness—of asking forgiveness of God and of other people, for example, and of forgiving others as well as oneself. In two places, the Big Book even implied that we should forgive and forget. Forget? Forget being beaten? Forget being sexually molested? Forget being neglected? Forget being publicly ridiculed and shamed? These childhood experiences were burned into my memory. Even if I could forgive those who had harmed me in these ways—and the Big Book, unfortunately, didn't tell me how to do that—I didn't think forgetting would be possible.

It turned out, however, that after 11 years in AA, I learned something about forgiving someone, and what forgiveness means. I learned this lesson by finding myself in a kind of do-or-die situation in which forgiving turned out to be the only good option available.

My mother had died suddenly and I had to return to my original home for her funeral. In the confusion of the next few days, one idea kept nagging at me: I would have to meet, I would have to be involved with, my father's sister, Aunt Margaret. Aunt Margaret! During my childhood, although she was sometimes kind to me (but there weren't many of those times), she was more often unkind, missing no opportunity to criticize me cruelly, even to the point of publicly embarrassing me. Negative in her attitude toward me, bullying, judgmental, insensitive, at times malicious—all of these came with Aunt Margaret! In my mind she'd become a living symbol of much of what my unhappy childhood involved. To have to deal with her—and I could no more avoid doing that than I could avoid going to my mother's funeral—was to raise the ghosts of an unhappy past.

Frankly, I didn't have the emotional or spiritual "energy" to handle Aunt Margaret on top of my own confused and conflicted feelings over my mother's death. "I don't know how I can do this," I said to my sponsor. "I don't know how I can handle the funeral, that whole crazy and sick family of mine, and Aunt Margaret at the same time!"

"Can you try to change the way you see her?" he asked. "Can you see her not as the tormentor of your childhood, but as a pathetic human being who has always wanted something she never got in your grandparents' alcoholic household—simply to be loved for herself? Can you reach around your own pain and touch her hurting spirit? Can you show love to her?"

"But I don't love her," I replied.

"I didn't ask you to love her," he said. "I'm suggesting that you act lovingly toward her, or at least try." I remember thinking: I can try—but it won't work.

I had no sooner arrived at my family's house, where I stayed during the funeral period, when the door opened and there was Aunt Margaret, an odd half-smile on her face. Here it is, I thought. This is it. God, give me some help with this. I went to her. "How kind of you to come," I said. "Thank you for doing this for me. It is very good of you." I hugged her close. (I didn't lie. Everything I said was true.) Aunt Margaret began to cry and I did too. She loved my mother and she was grieving. The old dragon was then just an old lady, perhaps frightened that her own death might not be very far away. Sometime later that evening, as she was leaving, I said to her, "I'm going to the funeral home tomorrow to make final arrangements. I'd really appreciate it if you'd come with me to help me through it." She readily agreed (was she surprised I had asked her?), and that established what was to be the pattern of my involvement with her over the next few days. I took opportunities to invite Aunt Margaret to be with me, whatever it was I was doing. I was signaling that I wanted to have her by my side. I was behaving lovingly.

Since then, seven years ago, there have been changes, significant ones I think, in our relationship. I call Aunt Margaret on Mother's Day and at Christmas and on her birthday. When her husband died suddenly, I called frequently. She writes me and I write back. No, she's still not my favorite person and it hasn't happened that I've come to like her, much less develop a warm, intimate relationship with her. Perhaps it never will. Perhaps too, it would be different if I were living near to her rather than across thousands of miles, and had to relate to her frequently and face-to-face. That might severely test my resolve to keep acting lovingly toward her! But the reality is that while memories of the past flicker from time to time, the pain of those memories is no longer there. The fire has gone out.

In all of this, Aunt Margaret never once asked for my forgiveness. Probably she doesn't know that she needs any forgiveness from me. So I've learned the surprising truth that I can forgive people even if they don't ask for my forgiveness, even if they don't realize that they need it. Forgiveness seems to depend more on the love of the one who does the forgiving than on the lovableness of the one being forgiven.

One last learning. I discovered that there is a meaning of remembering that goes beyond its minimal sense of just being able to recall. To remember in this sense means to refuse to let go—to keep something from the past alive, to give it weight in the here-and-now. In that sense, I no longer remember the pain Aunt Margaret caused me. I've forgotten it.

Jamie C.
West Henrietta, New York

Made Direct Amends
September 1979

After I had been in the Fellowship four and a half years, my brother invited me to visit him at his home in Ohio. I had been invited before, but I had doubts about my acceptance into his home, because of my track record. Our initial meeting after five years apart had me more nervous than the first time I spoke from an AA podium. The kangaroos in my tummy were having a real feisty boxing match.

All the way to Ohio, I kept going over some of the key personality flaws I have trouble with—chiefly my ability to open my mouth before engaging my brain. On the flight, I promised myself that no matter what I found disagreeable in my brother's way of life, I would keep my mouth shut—I also promised myself that I would make amends to him and to his wife. When the wheels hit the tarmac at Cleveland airport, the Serenity Prayer kept slipping through my mind.

My brother and I had long talks about everything. We hit it off like two long-lost pals. Of course, I was smart enough not to drag him through all the sordid details of my past. I talked about what had happened when I was with him. I was deeply surprised to find he had been doing his homework about the Fellowship and alcoholism. He had watched me trip down Rummy Lane and said that he had done the opposite of what I had done. He felt that because of watching me, he had not used booze or drugs as a means of escaping from the realities of his problems.

In taking Step Nine, it turned out, I was walking across a bridge that had already been built by my Higher Power, time and sobriety.

My sister-in-law was receptive to my amends, but not in a verbal form such as, "Yes, I understand." Her acceptance of me—my past and present—was silent. At first, it made me feel very uneasy. I felt as if I were being watched to see if my actions matched my words. I had to consider that these people had two small children, so I expect some of her motherly fears were blooming.

For the first few days, I walked softly and minded my Ps and Qs. I became slightly schizo, jabbering and loosening up with my brother and being careful around my sister-in-law. On the third day, I knew I had been accepted when she asked me to carry my 18-month-old niece to the car. Halfway to the car, I got a little nervous about dropping her (as a 33-year-old bachelor, I do not get too much practice carrying babies). When we got to the car, I turned the wee one over to Mother with a sigh of relief.

In their own ways, they had accepted my amends. On the flight back to my home in Florida, I felt very good about the trip and my Ninth Step. Of course, I had attended two meetings for reinforcement while in Ohio. That, coupled with a healthy dose of Step Eleven, made the trip a success.

R. B.
Fort Myers, Florida

Made Direct Amends
June 1990

"No, never! I'm willing to make amends to everyone on my list, but not to her. Not to Janice. Not after the terrible things she said to me. She called me a gold digger! She tried to turn her father and sisters and brother against me! As far as I'm concerned, she owes me an amends!"

As I finished my hostile outburst, my sponsor smiled sweetly with her exasperating, all-knowing look. "You may not be ready to make amends now," she said. "But there will come a time when you want to make amends to Janice. When you are spiritually ready, your Higher Power will find the right time and place. You'll make your amends, and you will feel wonderful. I promise you, it will happen."

I didn't believe her. I couldn't imagine why I would ever make amends to a person who had insulted and offended me. Janice lived a thousand miles away and that was as close as I wanted her to come.

At 30, Janice was my husband's oldest daughter. She had suffered terribly when her mother suddenly died of a cerebral hemorrhage. Her grief was so intense that she wrung a promise from her father never to remarry and to keep the family home exactly as her mother had left it. She was a devoted (although bossy) sister to her younger siblings. Talented, educated, beautiful, she was the mother of an adopted son and a devoted member of her church.

I was told that she had many fine qualities, but no matter. She didn't like me and I didn't like her. She took her father's marriage as a breach of promise and vowed never to forgive him or me. When I tried to win her over, she angrily blamed me for alienating her from her family. She wouldn't listen to my drunk apologies and belligerent fuming. She didn't understand that as a newlywed, I needed time (and plenty of alcohol) to adjust to my new status. It was all her fault! Then, somewhere during the last seven years of my drinking, she stopped telephoning. All communication between Janice and her family stopped.

But my sponsor was right. The time would come when I could hardly wait to make my amends. Making those amends would show the power of Step Nine to heal old wounds and unite loved ones.

By 1986, no one had seen or talked to Janice for almost seven years. She had stopped telephoning her father or the sister and brother who still lived with us. She never tried to contact her other sister, married and living in another state. Instead, she held on tightly to her grudges.

It was a family of grudge-holders. Her grandfather had gone to his grave without speaking to his brother for over 30 years. Her grandmother had refused to speak to her son's ex-wife for over 20. If you offended once, you were never forgiven. Old slights were recalled and thrown in your face. No one in the family knew how to say, "I'm sorry." No one ever admitted he or she might be wrong.

Into this family I came—a practicing alcoholic on the final downward plunge. I added my own flaming resentments to the troubles. I covered up my excesses by blaming the family. I drank the alcoholic's bitter brew of anger, resentment and bewildering despair. In the end, I alienated my stepfamily completely.

That stepfamily was the primary target of my Eighth Step. I was two years sober when I wrote my list and made those first, difficult direct amends. With newfound humility and dignity, I recognized my part in the angry scenes and hostile home atmosphere. I admitted my mistakes, as best I remembered them. I said those unfamiliar words, "I'm sorry," and I asked for forgiveness. I told each person what I was doing to turn my life around and promised that I would try my best not to offend again. I never mentioned the other person's behavior; I kept to my side of the street.

My husband and my stepchildren were astonished. No one had ever talked to them that way. No one had ever admitted his or her own weakness or failings before. The pattern of blame, excuses and grudge-holding had left no room for human error or compassion. Miraculously, everyone accepted my amends with grace and goodwill. But the real miracle was that they began to realize that they could do the same thing toward those whom they had offended. Making my amends set an example in human relations that would be invaluable in the tragic years ahead.

As I saw and felt the healing power of Step Nine, I began to sense true peace of mind. I began to feel right with the world and right with myself. As I crossed off the names on my Eighth Step list and made my amends to each person, I felt stronger, more secure, more in harmony with myself and others.

But something in me kept telling me I had more work to do. I looked at my list again and realized that Janice's name wasn't even on it. I had totally blanked her out of my mind—and out of my recovery.

As I reviewed my drinking behavior, I saw my motives more clearly. I had interfered between Janice and her father. I had contributed whole-heartedly to family arguments. I had alienated Janice purposely— to keep her from intruding into my life and to protect my right to drink as I wished. She had reacted with hurt anger, which let me justify my own self-serving actions. Seeing my own motives so clearly helped me understand the emotional and psychological stress my disease had created.

Now I wanted more than anything to clear away my guilt. I had reached the point my sponsor talked about: the point of spiritual readiness to work Step Nine completely. Now those 1000 miles seemed like an impenetrable distance. I asked my Higher Power to help me find a way to make direct amends.

That summer, my husband and I went on vacation to Lake Havasu, Arizona. Soaring desert temperatures became too hot to endure. As we searched the map for a place to cool off, we realized that Southern California was only a one-day drive away. Janice lived near Los Angeles. We telephoned ahead to ask whether our visit would be welcome. Surprisingly, Janice seemed pleased. I now believe that she was as sick of grudges and bitter memories as we were.

Our visit turned out to be a delightful success. For everyone, it was time to bury the past and start over. On the final day of our visit, I asked Janice if I could speak to her privately. In a very sweet and loving manner, she listened while I explained about my disease and how it had affected our relationship. I told her about AA and how the Fellowship was helping me change my life. And I assured her that I would do everything possible to bring the two sides of our family back together. She paused for a few moments, then hugged me warmly and said, "I think what you're doing is wonderful, and I'm proud of you. Now maybe we can be friends." With those words, the past was gone. We could begin again.

For the next two years, family relationships healed. Janice and her father forgave each other and telephoned frequently. Her brother and his wife and children spent two vacations with Janice's family. Her younger sister moved to California and lived with Janice for six months. Although our relationship was cordial, it wasn't the kind of warm, supportive relationship I enjoyed with my AA friends. But I was happy that we were at least speaking.

Then, in January 1988, Janice telephoned to tell us awful news. She had ovarian cancer. At that moment, our friendship changed. Janice asked for my support, and I was completely willing to give everything I had to help her.

During the next 12 months, Janice endured two surgeries and eight chemotherapies. She lost her long, thick hair. She lost weight and muscle. She lost the socially active life she loved. But she never lost her faith. She was an inspiration to me, and I to her. Through the grace of my Higher Power and the lessons I have learned in AA, I was able to share my experience, strength and hope—and help Janice keep a positive, faith-filled trust.

Janice's family rallied around her. Old grudges were forgotten. She and I talked at least twice a week every week for 12 anxious months. Her brother talked to her as much, or more, than I did. Her sisters prayed, and they gave as much support and encouragement as they could. My husband and I sent cards and flowers whenever she went into the hospital. We drove our motor home out to California twice and camped out on the street in front of her house. When Janice was joyfully pronounced "cured," we drove out a third time to celebrate.

Warm, loving, bubbling with life, Janice talked about the future the same way a starving person talks about food. She longed for life, for happiness, for wellness. But six months later, she was dead. A recurrence in the lower intestine. Colostomy. More chemotherapy. Wasting away. Finally, peace.

I still don't understand the terrible grief I feel. But I understand this: Because of the spiritual power of Step Nine, I have no regrets where Janice is concerned. The family that wept together in that flower-laden church would not have been there if Step Nine had not worked its healing magic. Making amends started a chain reaction of forgiveness that changed a whole family.

As my sponsor promised me years ago, I learned more from that one amends—the one I swore I'd never make—than from any other person or event in my recovery.

Carol S.
Albuquerque, New Mexico

From At Wit's End

February 2009

Heard at Meetings: "I had a really good reason for working Step Nine and making amends to my family and friends: I didn't want a parade of people at my funeral singing, Ding, dong, the wicked witch is dead!"

Carol K.
Sarasota, Florida

A Quiet Hatred

September 2003

I got sober in the spring of 1999, after a fruitless battle with drugs and alcohol that almost destroyed my life, family, and career. I was blessed with the "kiss of sobriety" the first night in the rehab center, when I got on my knees and asked God to take over my life. After a short stint in detox and aftercare, I started going to AA meetings in my hometown, found a sponsor and started working the Steps, just as I was directed to do.

My wife was a reluctant witness to my recovery at first, but over time our marriage started to come back together. I had done much damage to both her and our son, including the lying, cheating, stealing and begging that married alcoholics can relate to. Of course, she had to see action before she began to believe in me again, and I am happy to say that, for the most part, our 12-year-old marriage is better than it was when we said "I do."

When I started working my Fourth Step, one of the people I wrote about was my father-in-law. He was a man who was adored by my wife when I met her. He and I seemed to get along fine, but when I asked him for his daughter's hand in marriage, he surprised us both by saying no. Not because I was a drunk—my alcoholism was well-hidden back then—but because I was black and they were white. He said that he just couldn't see telling his friends that his daughter was married to a black man, and he did not attend our wedding. This devastated my wife. Everyone else from her side of the family attended our wedding, even my father-in-law's mother, but he didn't, and my wife could not forgive him for that.

All communication between the two of them ceased after we got married. I stayed out of it. We didn't even talk about him. Even as my drinking got worse, and when I left home for two years, they never communicated. So by the time I began working the Steps, they had not spoken to each other for over 10 years.

As I was working on my Eighth Step, my sponsor suggested that I write my father-in-law a letter. So I did. I had to think long and hard about what I had done that I had to make amends for, and I prayed to God to show me my part. As I wrote, I began by saying that I was sorry for encouraging my wife not to communicate with him, and for harboring ill will toward him. I told him that even though I hadn't specifically told my wife not to talk to him, I hadn't specifically said that she could. I realized that she was trying to protect her marriage, and me, and that I was happy she didn't have a relationship with him. While writing, I began to see how much I had secretly hated him for what he did to her, even though I had done much worse. I asked for his forgiveness and for us to move on from the past and restart our relationship.

Two weeks later, I received a letter from him. He started by thanking me for sending the nice letter, but he said that he would not accept my apology. He said that I didn't need to apologize—that he did. He wrote that he was so happy that I had written the letter, that he was wrong for what he had done, and that he would call soon. One week later, he called and talked to my wife for the first time in 11 years. They both cried so much that day, and so did I.

Since that time, my father-in-law has talked with us at least once a month and we are making plans for a visit soon. He even has established a great relationship with my 9-year-old son. He recently talked with my son for over an hour about baseball and has sent him some of his old baseball cards. This from a man my son has never met.

My wife says to me from time to time, "Thank you so much for what you did to bring back my father." I tell her it's one of the many gifts of sobriety, and then I call my sponsor and thank him again for telling me to write a letter.

Keith W.
Oceanside, California

A Tough Climb
August 2016

I had been in the program a number of years, but I still had a particular resentment for my son-in-law. He was a drinker and a smoker, and I didn't think he was a nice man. I had asked my daughter before Christmas what gift she wanted. She told me that she would like for me and Jeff, her husband, to get along.

In AA I learned to pray for people I didn't like, even when I didn't want to. I had been praying for him: "God bless the jerk." But now I really had to pray sincerely. I started saying the Eleventh Step prayer. I prayed that he would receive the same things I wished for my daughter, including compassion, understanding and peace.

My daughter's birthday falls in January. She invited me to her home for her birthday party. She lived in the country, about 25 miles out of town, in a trailer park located in a very poor area. I really hated going out there because I was the kind of mother-in-law who disliked everything my son-in-law did. I would sit in the corner feeling very hostile and finding fault with everything he did.

The day I went to their home for the birthday, we had a snowstorm. I couldn't drive up their hill, so I parked and started to climb this quarter-mile-long hill with cake in one hand and gift in the other. About five inches of snow covered the ground. I had come straight from work and it was a difficult climb.

Suddenly, I noticed two men walking down the hill toward me. "Hey, Mom," one called. It was my son. With him was Jeff, my son-in-law. They had come to help me up the hill. It was a very steep hill and I was sliding and falling in the snow. All of a sudden, we started acting silly and throwing snowballs. One of them would pull me and one would push me and we were laughing so hard I was out of breath.

By the time we got to their trailer, I wasn't angry. We were laughing and joking. For the first time, I felt comfortable in their home. Jeff grilled steaks outside on their little porch. We had a nice time.

On the way home I thought, first, about how this prayer stuff really does work and second, I realized I played a part in my hostile relationship with Jeff. I had contributed to the anger and fear. I had carried anger and resentment with me every time I walked through their door. I brought it with me. No matter what was going on between my daughter and Jeff, I was the one carrying all this garbage with me.

I knew then that I had to make amends. So one day, I walked up to Jeff and said I was wrong. I apologized for adding fuel to the fire and asked whether there was something I could do to make things right.

He gave me a suggestion. I had been bringing food and clothes and toys over every time I visited. As he saw it, I had been taking over his job of providing for his family and taking away some of his dignity. By admitting my part, we were both able to find healing.

About a year later, Jeff was working on a roofing project when he took a bad fall. He became paralyzed from the neck down. I was so thankful that I had made amends before his accident because if I had waited, it would have been an apology brought about by pity. I don't think he would have accepted it.

He survived for five years after the fall. During that time, we got closer. We were never buddy-buddy, but we could look each other in the eye with respect. We had many talks about religion and our Higher Powers. He was so afraid of dying and I was able to tell him about the God of my understanding that I had come to know through AA.

Jeff never stopped drinking or smoking. But I had learned how to love someone I had once hated. I could see healing on both sides. When he died I was there, in the corner, sending him all the love and peace I could. In AA, I was given the knowledge and desire to pass on what I had been given. I was so grateful to send it to him.

L.A.
St. Louis, Missouri

CHAPTER FIVE

Exes: Finally Divorced From the Pain

———————◇———————

The guilt and shame of past relationships can still run—and
ruin—a life, until Step Nine changes everything

I f there were a universal questionnaire sent out to find the main
reason for relationship breakups, we think we know the answer.
Until we gather the courage to stand before our exes offering our
amends for our alcoholic behavior, we will be bound to those old loves
in a relationship of guilt and shame. And the deeper our shame and
guilt about the effects of alcohol on our relationships, the more challenging our amends will be.

In the following stories, our members—very often with the strong
support of sponsors—succeed in walking peacefully away from their
exes for the very first time, often after decades of shared, haunting pain.

Douglas M. tells us in the story "Alone with My Ex," that after he
hadn't spoken to his former wife in 20 years, his first attempt at an
amends resulted in her screaming at him to leave. When their son's
prayers convinced him to try again, he bravely did, and the healing
was amazing. In "Captain Chaos," Skitch F. stayed close to a wonderful sponsor, made a difficult amends, and learned that "people and relationships, my part in them, and how I treat others, are important
in my life." And the anonymous writer of "Peace With the Past," says
he was never a happy drunk. But since putting Step Nine to work, he
writes, "Thank God for AA. It saved my life, then taught me how to live
without regret."

25 Years of Regret
September 2013

I got sober in 2006 after more than 25 years of drinking. During that time I left quite a path of destruction in my wake, not the least of which were three failed marriages. I was rarely capable of an honest and emotionally healthy relationship. That's not to say that I was always the cause of these relationships coming to an end. There was usually enough blame to go around, but I certainly was not the easiest person to live with.

I was married for the first time at age 22. Let's call her Dawn. She was my first love and it was all very exciting. We were engaged for nearly two years and had plans for a long and happy life together. Shortly after getting married, the relationship went terribly wrong and ended. One Saturday afternoon, Dawn began the process of moving out. Her sister (let's call her Liz) was there to help her move. I was less than accommodating and did my best to make the process as unpleasant as possible. I don't remember everything that transpired, but I do recall attempting to throw them both out of the apartment. Like any big sister, Liz was determined to stand up for her younger sibling. We began to argue, and I immediately started yelling.

What I said cannot be printed here. I reached deep and pulled out every curse and derogatory term I could summon. I proceeded to call Liz the worst names I could think of, names I would not want anyone to say to my sister, or my daughter or any woman. It was shameful.

I didn't see or hear from Liz or Dawn for nearly 25 years, until it was time to make amends. I made contact with Dawn and we eventually talked on the phone. I told her I was sober and that I wanted to make amends to her. She told me she was in Al-Anon and that she understood. She said she owed me an amends as well.

We shared stories about our kids, and we laughed and even cried a little. I told her that she would always hold a special place in my heart. It was corny, but true. I asked Dawn if it would be OK for me to reach out to her sister. She said that Liz would probably enjoy hearing from me. I wasn't so sure about that, but I said thank you.

So I wrote Liz an email. I told her that I had been sober for a while, and that I had been doing my best to be a better person. I apologized for all of the hateful things I said to her that day. I didn't make any excuses. I said I was wrong and deeply sorry.

Liz wrote back and said she was happy for me, but didn't have any idea as to what I was talking about. She appreciated me reaching out and was glad to hear that Dawn and I connected, but she didn't remember me saying anything hateful. She had completely forgotten that day. Her response amazed me. I had carried the shame and guilt of that day for more than 25 years, and she didn't even remember it! Worse, all this time I'd been continuously suppressing the negative feelings from that and many other instances with the help of alcohol.

I'm pleased to know that Liz didn't carry any hurt from my actions; I'm happy that she moved on. It's also humbling to realize that I don't always play as important a role in other people's lives as I think. Liz didn't give me much thought for 25 years. Why should she? She didn't hate me or want revenge. On the other hand, I regretted the things I'd said. I felt bad for 25 years and never did one thing to correct it, until I found AA.

Today I know that if I do or say something that may cause harm to another person, I have to make amends immediately. I don't want shame and guilt to lead me back to a way of life that I gave up six years ago. I have to let go of these feelings, and I can do that if I work the Ninth Step to the best of my ability.

Richard V.
Charlotte, North Carolina

Unexpected Dividends
August 1988

I was feeling some pressure to see my ex-mother-in-law, Libby. I had not seen her for the 10 years I had been divorced. Last June, I learned that she was in a nursing home and had not spoken for seven years. The Ninth Step says that this process of making amends is for me. It was clear that I could not get anything from her.

With my sponsor, I prepared what I would do. In this Step, as with all parts of the program, I do not act alone. We decided that I would read to Libby and leave her an artificial plant. The main point was to make amends for abandoning her 10 years previously. When I left my husband, I was not able to say goodbye to any member of his family. Now I needed to mend this hole in my spirit.

Two program friends from New York City went with me. The town was 30 miles north of Scranton, Pennsylvania. We combined the trip with a chance to see the fall colors. I needed to renew my heart as well as my spirit.

I arrived in the small town and decided to get it over with and make the visit immediately. I left my two friends shopping while I visited Libby. I bought a small plant and prepared to enter the nursing home.

As I went through the door, I glanced over my left shoulder. My surprise stunned me so that my knees buckled beneath me. My ex-husband drove up that instant. His second wife and child got out of the car and passed me down the hall. My first alcoholic impulse was to run and hide in the women's room. Then I said, "God, if you have given me this opportunity, the least I can do is to go through with it."

I walked out the door into the parking lot. I tried to make my voice sound casual as if I spoke to Bill each day. I had not seen him for 10 years. He came from Philadelphia and I from New York. Here we were meeting at the same time and place, 10 years later.

I had written him about 18 months previously to make amends. For whatever reason, he did not respond. Now I had the chance to do it in person.

As I spoke, Bill turned. His astonishment was as great as mine. He had to do his recovery in public. He observed, "Seeing you is like seeing someone I went to high school with." I thought that was an appropriate way to put me back in his life. It was so very long ago. I was not able to make any fancy speeches. We were both too surprised. "I wrote you that letter about my alcoholism because I wanted you to know what went wrong with our marriage. I was so sick and crazy." He smiled a thin smile and said, "I also remember the good times. I have no regrets." A small word to lift such a burden from my heart. My arms did not know how heavy was the rock until I put it down. We made a few more attempts at conversation. He with his potted plant in his arms and I with my artificial plant clutched in my hand. This was the most intimate moment in our 10 years of marriage. He truly saw me for who I am—a drunk. I did not have to pretend to him or to the world. What a relief! I decided to let him visit with his family. I went back to town and told my friends of the miracle that had happened. Only God could have brought us together over so many miles and so many years.

The next day, I went to see Libby. She lay quietly in the bed, never stirring. Are we really sure that unconscious people do not know us? My sister reminded me before I went to act as if Libby could hear everything. I told her about my disease and how it made me act in ways I did not value. I regretted that I had not said goodbye before and told her I had come to do that step now. I read the first chapter of Hannah Hurnard's *Hinds' Feet on High Places*. It is the story of a woman named "Much-Afraid" who is transformed by her relationship with The Shepherd.

Truly that is what is happening to me in the process of this Step. The Promises do come true before we are halfway through.

Ann D.
New York, New York

Early Amends
(From Dear Grapevine)
August 2009

I never thought I could stay sober for a year in the program. So when I heard about Steps Eight and Nine in a Step meeting, I thought, How wonderful!

Step Nine was so compelling to me. I believed so much in the program and was so happy I was able to put four months together. I had been told in the rooms, "We must work our own program." So I told my wife I was sorry for all I had done and put her through. I told her how much I loved her and wanted to be with her and how grateful I was that she'd stayed with me.

I wrote a letter of amends to my first wife on her birthday, a letter she never acknowledged. I cried on my daughter's shoulder. She said, "That's OK, Dad. It wasn't that bad." I went to my parents' graveside to make amends to them; I heard myself say, "Thank you."

It was all one of those wonderful, common miracles that come our way in the program. My wife died the next year. I was still working Step Four. I think now I would never have been given the gift, or the opportunity, of having the memory of making amends to my wife, if I had waited to do the Twelve Steps in sequence.

Jim R.
Skokie, Illinois

Captain Chaos
September 2007

I made up my own definition for the word "freebie" when I was in my late teens and already an alcoholic. The word described when I got out of doing something I really didn't want to do, but didn't want anyone to know it. For instance, if someone else had to cancel a meeting that I didn't want to show up for—it was a "freebie." Not only did I get out of it, but I also got credit for doing something I didn't do. Does that make sense?

Then along came sobriety, the Steps and my sponsor. My sponsor said, "You better do a Fifth before you pick up a fifth." I did my Fifth Step right before my first anniversary. Although it took months for me to do Steps Six and Seven (a story of its own involving stealing but finally making it through the grocery store without grazing), I finally got to Steps Eight and Nine. My first wife was on my list of amends. When the kids were teenagers, we'd gotten divorced after being married for over 17 years. When I was coming up on a couple years of sobriety, I went to see her to make amends. She said, "Oh, I know what you're going to do. I'm just glad you're sober, and you don't have to do this." The book says we don't push anyone who doesn't want it. Wow, I thought, a great big freebie.

Years of sobriety followed this experience, and it was not a bad life by any means, especially compared to the life I'd lived as a drunk. I kept my sponsor, even when his company gave him a new assignment and he moved. I became friends with Jim P. If I couldn't reach my sponsor, Jim was there. He was an active old-time Twelfth-Stepper. I still had a big resentment about my first marriage, and Jim said I needed to pray that she'd get the things I wanted for myself. I said that she'd already gotten all my things (money and material things). But he said he was also talking about security, peace of mind, and in general, the things I'd robbed myself and my family of in my years of alcoholic terrorism. I'd pray, because I believed Jim, but I didn't have faith in a Higher Power. Things changed, but very slowly.

Five more years passed. One day I was talking to my sponsor about a problem I was having. Before I finished, he said, "Tell me about your Ninth Step with your first wife." Whoa. I said, "This problem has nothing to do with that." I reminded him that my first wife said that she didn't want to hear it. He replied, "We need to work on it now." He said I needed to do a Ninth Step with my first wife.

There was a lot of work for me to do. I had to list the nature of the harms I had done—the miserable life in our home as a result of my alcoholic drinking. I was unpredictable and kept the house in turmoil. My family even had a name for me: Captain Chaos. Pretty flattering, huh? The things I'd taken from the family were the things that, years before, Jim had told me to pray about. My sponsor and I talked about it every week for a few months.

Finally, I was ready. We decided that I was going to ask her to have lunch with me. My daughter was having a party for one of my grandkids in a couple of weeks. My sponsor said while we were all at the party, I could ask my first wife to go to lunch. When the day arrived, there just wasn't the right opportunity. I looked across the room and saw my first wife and her new husband opening the door to leave. I yelled out her name and asked, "Will you go to lunch with me?" The whole room took a breath and stood still, waiting for her reply. "Sure. Give me a call," she said.

Two weeks later, in a restaurant, I made a real Ninth Step amends, and she listened. Things aren't the greatest between us, but we can at least speak civilly to each other. The amends helped my now-adult kids and grandkids, too.

First Jim, and then my sponsor, taught me with their experience, strength and hope, about what is important in life, what the book *Twelve Steps and Twelve Traditions* says at the start of Step Eight. "Steps Eight and Nine are concerned with personal relations." People and relationships, my part in them and how I treat others, are important in my life. Jim used to say, "When I came to AA, I loved things and used people. But since I've been in AA, I've learned to love people and use things." Jim passed a month short of 53 years of sobriety a few years ago. He taught me so much.

With the help of AA, my sponsor and Jim, I've come to realize how expensive a "freebie" can be. To know "a new freedom and a new happiness," I need to watch out for that easier, softer way that can distract me from working the Steps of Alcoholics Anonymous.

Skitch F.
Albuquerque, New Mexico

Scene of the Crime
September 1993

The rocks looked the same. The light in the sky at sunset was as I remembered it; the stillness and silence of the pinyon-juniper forest had not changed. This was the day I returned to the windswept landscape of northern Arizona from which I had fled five years before.

When I left, I was running from my alcoholism. I went 4,000 miles north of this land of open skies and silence, only to find that my disease came the distance with me. Once into recovery, I stayed where I had landed, building a foundation through the Twelve Steps of Alcoholics Anonymous for a life of sobriety and serenity.

But I knew, during the years I stayed in Alaska, that I would one day return to the scene of my crimes, for I had an amends to make there. So I found myself, during a vacation in the Southwest, driving the familiar road toward my old home. The time had finally come to face a ghost from the past.

In Sedona, I passed that same laundromat where the violence had first erupted, back in 1981. I should have left him then, but I didn't. There were a million reasons for me to stay, but the most important was that he was my drinking buddy, my provider. We drank and battled and made up for three more stormy years after the laundromat scene. I had been too fearful to leave him, too addicted to turn my back. The heart-pounding fear of his violent nature came back to me as I drove through town. I found the nearest meeting.

Appropriately, the topic of the meeting was fear. When I was called on, I told the group that I was going to make amends to a man I feared; I confessed it was possible that he might hit me again, or worse. Although five years had passed since I had escaped from him, I was not at all convinced that he would greet me warmly. Nevertheless, the amends had to be made. Step Nine said that I had to admit to him where I was wrong. I chose to do this face-to-face.

A man sitting across the table from me spoke next. "Fear keeps a lot of us from making amends," he said. "But I have found no other way to resolve those conflicts which arise from the harm we do to others. You can face the man with courage." He smiled at me. "Courage is fear that has said its prayers."

In Flagstaff the next morning, I sat in a restaurant where I had sat a hundred times before, drinking coffee with shaky hands. The ghosts were moving and talking to me from the walls, and the fearful part of me wanted to run away again. I prayed for courage and went on.

Closer still to my old stomping grounds, I stopped the car along the highway, deciding to walk a couple of miles to reach a volcano crater. I hiked along, lost in my own thoughts, hearing voices from the past. Once over the lava wall, I entered the volcano crater quietly. An eerie wind blew, creating jet stream highways for the birds and sweeping the air clean. The sun passed behind a tall spire of rock at noon and a shadow fell across my lap.

The volcano crater was a place of stillness and meditation. Five years before, I had come to this same place to make the decision to leave the Southwest for Alaska. I had felt at once terrified and aroused by the prospect of a major change. On that fateful day, lacking the perspective of distance and sobriety, I had taken a long look at my life and made a guess about the best path to take.

I remembered these things now, as I admired the silhouette of a big old ponderosa pine against the curve of volcanic basalt. And I asked again for the courage to go back to face the man I had hurt by my choice of paths.

Later that afternoon, I cruised slowly through the neighborhood in which he and I had once lived. I looked at each little wood house for a clue as to which was his. Part of me secretly hoped he would no longer be there. When I saw it, I drove past, backed up, pulled into the driveway, and then very nearly pulled back out. His car was there. Children's toys littered the yard. His name was on a sign next to the door.

Maybe he's at work, I thought, panicking. Maybe his wife doesn't want me around. My feet walked toward the door of their own accord. My heart was pounding. My face stung as though he had already slapped me.

When he came to the door, he recognized me immediately. With only a slight hesitation, he invited me in, introduced me to his children and offered me a chair. Visibly nervous, I told him I couldn't stay long, but that I had some things to say.

He went to get a beer, offered me one. I suddenly wondered what I was doing there. His home was a slippery place. Sending up another quick prayer for my Higher Power to put the right words in my mouth, I began to speak.

"I've come to tell you what happened when I left you," I said. "I told you I'd come back. I was lying to you when I made that promise, because I knew in my heart that I was never going to return. My disappearance hurt you, and I apologize for that."

He began to protest, to rewrite that five-year-old piece of history, to tell me how it happened. I had to interrupt him and ask him to let me have my say; for a moment, it felt like old times, me arguing with him about the facts.

"I am sober now," I told him, "and it's important for me to come back here and tell you that the problems we had in our relationship were at least 50 percent my fault. I always blamed you for everything—for my alcoholism, for my failures, for my misery. Those things were not your fault. You were good to me in many ways."

He didn't know how to answer me. So instead he drank some more beer and asked about my family. As I sat in that man's living room I watched his stature diminish before my eyes. No longer was he a cruel and vengeful lunatic. No longer did he possess the power to terrify me. He was just a man with an alcohol problem. The moment I saw him for what he was, I could forgive him, for his problem was no different than mine. He just hadn't found a solution yet. He wasn't looking for a solution yet. I asked my Higher Power to be with him, and all the anger and fear dissolved into pity for a man still battered by his disease.

Soon I got up and prepared to leave. I thanked him for taking the time to listen to what I had to say. Shyly, he stuck out his hand toward me. I grasped it, then impulsively stepped forward and hugged him.

I drove away from the house without looking back. My shoulders felt light, as if a giant weight had been lifted. Until it was lifted, I hadn't even been aware it was there.

The tortured autopsies I had performed on that relationship were finally behind me. For the first time, I was able to let him go. He did not hit me. He did not seduce me. His power over me was broken at last.

I enjoyed a buoyancy of spirit after that visit. By admitting where I was at fault, I was given the ability to forgive a man who had held me in bondage for years after I had left him. With forgiveness came a freedom that I had not anticipated. The amends had required nothing but courage, and a faith that my Higher Power would carry me where I had been too afraid to walk alone.

Kit K.
Sterling, Alaska

Alone With My Ex
September 2010

I had been sober around six months, and one day my daughter came to a meeting. She said, "I'm going out to visit Mom. I want you to come with me." I had not spoken to my ex-wife in over 20 years. So I really did not know what to expect.

When we arrived at the house my ex-wife was in the yard working. When she saw me she did not speak to me. She spoke to our daughter, but the words were for me. She screamed. "I don't want to see that man. I don't want to hear anything he has to say. And if he doesn't leave my property, I'll call the police."

I left there very angry, vowing never to return. The memory of our separation and divorce returned. She had been awarded the kids, house, car, furniture and anything else of value. I was locked up in jail, could not appeal in court and received nothing.

When I returned home I called my sponsor. He said, "Just do AA and leave the rest in God's hands." He reminded me that I had made a commitment when I took the Third Step. "Let Go and Let God," he said.

My sponsor got me busy doing service work, chairing meetings, speaking and going on Twelfth Step calls with him. He was also with me as I did Steps Four through Nine.

When I'd been sober around 16 months, my youngest son called. We had talked and written to one another while he was in school, and he had now returned home to stay. He said he wanted to see me; I said OK. We met after a meeting and he said, "We are going out to visit Mom."

I told him what had transpired the last time I had seen his mother. I let him know that I was not going to go through that again. He replied, "It's OK, Dad. I talked to Mom and she said it would be OK." I said a prayer, we left the clubhouse, and I returned to the home I once owned. I had not been inside the house for over 22 years.

Within a short period of time I found myself alone with my ex in the living room. Then something happened. Instead of an awkward silence, my mouth opened and out came Step Nine. I apologized for my past actions (never mentioning anything she had done). I asked her what I could do to atone for my past behavior.

She said, "Treat your children like a father should. And continue to do whatever it is that you're doing."

On the way home my son said, "Dad, I have prayed for a long time that one day you and Mom would just speak to one another. But I had given up. I knew how Mom was, and you were still drinking. However, when I saw you and Mom talking and laughing I knew it was a miracle and I was filled with a great happiness." Tears of joy flowed from my eyes. I realized that God had done for me what I could not have done for myself.

Today, I still remember that day. And the countless other days over the past 15 years when all I needed to do was to "Let Go and Let God" work his miracles.

Douglas M.
Covington, Kentucky

Peace With the Past
September 1995

I have had many beautiful experiences in my 10 years of sobriety in the program. The most beautiful of all: a Ninth Step amends I made to my college girlfriend, Mary Beth.

Mary Beth and I had an on-again, off-again relationship throughout our four years of college. We met during freshman year and fell in love immediately. You'd have to have been 18, lonely, and homesick to understand how important she was to me. But my drinking and emotional instability, my difficulty in imagining her point of view and giving consideration to her, did us in by the end of the year.

Sophomore year we tried again, with similar results. Then in the middle of our junior year, I sobered up for the first time, and things looked better for us. But that summer I drank again, and when I returned to school that fall I became irritated with her, blaming my increasing unhappiness on shortcomings I imagined in her. Once again, Mary Beth and I broke up.

I stopped drinking only a month after starting up, for even I could see the change alcohol made in my temperament and outlook. I was never a happy drunk; I was usually mean and ornery. I even tried AA that fall. But I didn't like it, so I quit after 30 days. Nobody was going to tell me how to stay dry. I could do it on my own.

But being dry wasn't enough, I found. After four months of not drinking, I was more lonely and frightened that I'd ever been in my life. And I was terribly confused: My first period of sobriety had gone so well, my life had turned around immediately—even though I wasn't in AA. Why not this time? I prayed to God to help me.

My prayer was answered. One day I happened to be with a group of people who were learning about organizations to help those who were down on their luck. An AA member was among those who spoke to us about their organizations. He seemed so happy, so peaceful. That had a big impact on me—it was such a contrast to my own misery and desperation.

I resolved then and there to give AA another try. I put it off for a week or two, of course, but finally I was so unhappy I did the unthinkable: I went to a meeting.

When I got there, I didn't know what to say. Everyone realized immediately I was a newcomer, so they held a First Step meeting. When it was my turn to speak, I tried to tell them how awful I felt, how lonely and desperate, how much I hated myself, but I couldn't. To my great embarrassment, I began to cry. I just couldn't help myself.

That was January 17, 1985. I've stayed sober and attended AA meetings ever since then. For the rest of the school year I clung to Mary Beth.

I tried to convince myself she felt the same way about me, although anyone could plainly tell her feelings for me were lukewarm at best.

It shouldn't have been a big surprise when I got a letter from her the following autumn telling me she wanted to cool it. She was in graduate school while I was still unemployed and aimless. The letter was devastating to me, and I responded as only an alcoholic can: I went into a rage of self-righteous indignation.

You know how people say you should write your feelings down in a letter, then tear it up? It is good advice. I didn't take it. After filling both sides of six pages with rage and accusations, I held the letter for three days, then mailed it.

I didn't hear from Mary Beth for a long, long time after that. Realizing my mistake, I sent her a halfhearted apology six months later. She didn't respond. Then I got it; in her book, I was a jerk.

A year went by, then another. I continued to stay sober, and my life changed dramatically for the better. Every now and then I thought of Mary Beth and felt bad about my behavior to her. I wrote more letters to her, and this time I didn't send them, believing that I had no right to intrude further on her life.

After five years of this, I still didn't feel at peace. Finally I realized something had to be done, so I wrote another letter to her. I described to Mary Beth the journey of my sobriety and all the changes it had brought to my life. I apologized with all my heart to her for the way I'd treated her, and I asked for her forgiveness. This time I mailed the letter.

She wrote me back within a week. On the outside of the envelope she wrote, "Peace with the past." Inside, she applauded the changes in me, told me how her life had gone—and gave me her forgiveness.

Not every amends has gone so well, but no matter whether it turned our well or badly, I've found each time the peace for which I searched. I'm no longer haunted by the memories of my mistakes and the injuries I inflicted on others. Thank God for AA. It saved my life, then taught me how to live it without regret.

Anonymous
Sheboygan, Wisconsin

CHAPTER SIX

Where the Guilt Runs Deep, So Can the Peace

———◇———

Nothing is more painful than sitting humbly before a victim of your crime … except avoiding that day

S ometimes we perceive the wreckage of our past as just too smoldering and smoking, too loaded with land mines, for us to safely deal with. But so many decades of sober experience have taught us that the courage to venture into our crime scenes with healing in mind is exactly what can bring us—and our victims—the miracle of peace.

In the first story of this chapter, "Giving a Little Bit Back," Michael P. escapes from prison and goes into a liquor store and shoots a clerk in the chest. After many years in prison, Michael locates the clerk in a convalescent home to make a long overdue amend. What happens is a moment Michael will never forget.

Step Nine can bring sober alcoholics the most enormous gifts. It's the reason why the anonymous writer of "Zipped Up Tight," can write, "Discovering AA was like a Christmas morning that wasn't going to end in a fight."

"The Amends I Most Dreaded to Make," by member D.S., and "A Letter from the Mother of the Man I Killed," by James B., are more about liberation than liability. So is Holly H.'s "Spiritual Agony," which tells us "Making amends to the murderer of a precious friend was the most terrifying prospect—next to taking another drink."

Giving a Little Bit Back
June 1997

On May 16, 1969, Bill (not his real name) arrived at a liquor store in Las Vegas, Nevada where he worked part-time. The extra money helped raise his small family. At age 32, he was young and doing pretty well. At 11:30 that night, all that changed. I changed it.

That day in May I was on escape from a southern prison. I'd made my way across the country, stealing, robbing, drinking and doing drugs. I'd been a fugitive for 22 days when my path and Bill's crossed. I walked into the liquor store with my gun out. My intention was to get money. Bill handed me the money, about $60 dollars. He was scared to death. I remember pulling the trigger. The heavy .38 caliber bullet hit him in the center of the chest.

A few minutes later, I was arrested. Bill was rushed into surgery. I was charged with attempted murder and robbery. At the county jail, a few hours after my arrest, a police officer told me, "If that clerk dies, you're gonna burn." I told the cop, "Burn me, sucker." That was the kind of person I was in those days.

Bill lived, through heroic efforts of the surgeons. He'd lost so much blood, however, that he was left permanently brain-damaged. It was as if he'd had a major stroke. Doctors told his family he would never be the same again.

I spent many years in prison. After my release, in January 1987, I made my way into AA. I haven't had a drink since.

A few months into sobriety, I was diligently working Step Nine. I mentioned Bill to my sponsor, and he suggested I look him up. He said I needed to do that. I called Las Vegas information. Bill had a common last name so there were several listings. On the third one, I made contact with his son. After I explained who I was and what I was doing, the son told me his father had been in a convalescent home in El Cajon, California for six years. I lived in El Cajon. I asked him where the hospital was. He told me it was six blocks from my house.

The next day I went to the hospital. I explained to the nurse who I was. She told me Bill was on the patio, and I went out, very scared to see him. He was in a wheelchair. He was 50 years old but looked much older. The nurse said he hadn't spoken in the six years he'd been there. Not one word. For the first time in my life, I saw before me the result of my alcoholic behavior. A totally crippled, mute human being. To say I was shaken is an understatement.

I sat next to Bill. I calmly told him who I was and why I was there. There was no response at all. I made as heartfelt an amend as I could. It shook me to my very soul. I got up to leave. I don't know why, but I leaned over and kissed Bill on the forehead. Then I saw the miracle. Bill looked right at me and said clearly, "Thank you for coming to see me." There was a tear in his eye.

The nurse was completely taken aback. She said it was the first thing he'd spoken in years. She was crying when I left. So was I.

I still recall that day in 1969 when I changed a man's life. I remember the day, nine years ago, when I got to make an amend to that man. For one moment that day, I felt the presence of God. If you have amends to make, please make them. I implore you—don't be afraid.

Michael P.
El Cajon, California

The Amends I Most Dreaded to Make
August 1977

I had made all my amends but one. I had faced my father, my mother, my brothers, my second ex-wife, and numerous employers and acquaintances I had stolen from or cheated. The results had been incredible. Every one of them was kind and appreciative of what I was trying to do with my life. Many of them told me, "If there's anything I can do for you, please let me know." The peace I was beginning to experience was astounding. I also kept a list of the people I wasn't able to locate, in case I should ever come into contact with them. Now there was no more rationalizing, no more amends to make in order to delay the one I dreaded most.

She was a pedestrian I ran down in September of 1965. She was rushed to the hospital with a brain hemorrhage and wasn't expected to live. There were investigators looking for me, and I kept avoiding them. When I was sent back to jail for the sixth and last time, I learned that she had been released from the hospital at her request and was returning to her home in Brussels, Belgium. That was all I knew. I had no idea what condition she was in. I didn't want to know. I was paying the price for my mistake in time behind bars. My debt was paid.

I had my last drink two years after the accident. I had just spent eight months trying to stay sober without those damn Steps, and the results had been nil. This time, I decided to give them a try. I had some difficulty understanding and coming to terms with some of the Steps in the beginning. I guess we all do. But eventually, the understanding came and the application followed.

Now, without realizing how far I'd come, I knew I had to face up to the one amends I had dreaded ever since I had come to comprehend Step Nine. That little voice inside me wouldn't let up. I had to do it.

I really didn't know where to start, where to find her. I looked at the police report, found her address in Belgium and wrote to her. The letter was returned: "Addressee Unknown." I called the Belgian consulate in Los Angeles. They told me there was nothing they could do, but that I might write the American embassy in Brussels. I did.

Then the news: "In response to your letter of April 27, 1972, I regret to inform you that Miss W__died in Belgium in 1966 shortly after her return from the United States. This information was provided to the embassy by her last known employer."

Oh my God, no! Not because of the accident. How would I know for sure? I was torn. Part of me was saying I had done all I could do and I would have to learn to accept it. But another part of me felt uneasy and unsettled. Then I realized that she must have had a family, and that I certainly owed them amends.

In her medical jacket at the hospital, I found the addresses of a sister in Canada and two doctors in Belgium. I wrote my letter of amends to the sister. It too came back: "Addressee Unknown." I wrote to both doctors in Belgium. Six months later, I received a reply from one of them. He commended what I was trying to do and sent the sister's address, in Belgium. I wrote my letter of amends again. In two weeks, I had a reply in Flemish. It took another week to have it translated.

> "This morning, we received your letter. I thank you with all my heart. Perhaps your letter helped to cure the deep wound that was caused by the death of my only, loved younger sister. Yes, she is dead following that accident. It was terribly hard. It still causes such a strong pain. We loved each other enormously. She was an artist; later, I shall send you a copy of one of her works.
>
> "The insurance concerning the accident was paid to us [the writer and her husband], the trip and the burial by us. We suffered financially terribly much because of her death. She helped us very much. She was a good person. She was so dear to me. A day does not go by without my thinking about her. We have one child, Julie, 8 years old. I am sending a picture taken on the day of her first communion.
>
> "We are not rich, but my husband and I are very happy together, and are taking care of everything together with love. We do not want to profit by you. You must pay nothing. If you want, and if you can, perhaps give something to put in Julie's savings account. She will remain alone in life sometimes. But you must not defraud yourself of anything. I would be completely glad about that—the money for the child. I am a schoolteacher, and I try to make a good person out of my child.
>
> "I keep your letter for Julie. And will you write a small letter off and on? That also I would like very much. And you must pray for

us and all those who have lost someone in an accident. It is so hard. Life is so short. I am so glad, so very glad that you have written. I am so thankful to you. I shall finish for now, for I must go to school. Julie also prays for you and sends her best regards. I hope you find someone who will translate the letter to you, because I don't know enough English. God is good and merciful, and we must be like that also. God bless you."

I did write again. The letters I received have been even warmer. I found it hard to believe and accept. How could anyone have that much love and forgiveness? Like most of my life in AA, it was too much to comprehend. Then we began to correspond about seeing each other some day and how nice it would be to sit face-to-face.

In July 1974, I flew to New York to meet my 9-year-old daughter, who was going with me to Belgium. This was at the suggestion of my ex-wife, and I was startled by her new trust in me. She was impressed that I had changed that much.

It was difficult for my daughter, leaving her mother for the first time. I hadn't seen her in three years, and never had it been just the two of us. On the plane, we had dinner and went to sleep. I woke up suddenly, just before we began our descent into Brussels, and she was standing over me, just looking at me. Then she was in my arms crying, and I felt for the first time in my life the overwhelming and beautiful responsibility of being a parent.

I don't have the words to describe our trip to Belgium. When we were met at the airport by our Belgian friends, we embraced and cried as if we had known one another for years. We lived in their home for two weeks. Our daughters were instant friends in spite of the language barrier. My daughter and I were given a grand tour of western Belgium. We crossed the English Channel from France to Dover. Everything was done for us. They fed us, washed our clothes, and introduced us to their friends. And when the girls had gone to bed, we spent many hours talking about the accident and its aftermath, talking and crying together. My daughter and I were loved in a way so total and so foreign to me that I thought there must be a catch. It scared the hell out of me. One day, they told me that if anything happened to them, I would have to come to Belgium and take care of everything. I was very flattered but had no concept of the depth of what they were saying until my final day there.

At five o'clock on the morning we were to leave Belgium, I awoke to find sitting at the foot of my bed the sister of the woman I killed in 1965. She was crying and looking at me intently. Then, very softly, she said, "You are my brother. My real brother. My very dear and real brother. Don't ever forget that."

I never have. I doubt that I ever will.

D. S.
Desert Hot Springs, California

Dream Becoming Reality
(From Dear Grapevine)
December 2009

Being incarcerated has many challenges. With nearly three years left on a 10-year sentence, I felt stuck on Step Nine. I believed I had to be face-to-face for an amends to be made. I felt that no one wanted a jailhouse letter saying, "I'm sorry."

When I brought this up to our AA volunteer, Harold, he reminded me that I had a disease that would kill me if I were not growing spiritually. He suggested that I start writing letters to the ones I had harmed.

I started right away and the result was my spiritual experience. All I needed was to be open-minded about how the amends needed to be made.

This program has not only given me a guide on how to live, but a hope for the life I've only dreamed about...even in prison!

Marc W.
Boonville, Missouri

A Letter From the Mother of the Man I Killed

December 2006

On February 20, 2001, while drinking and driving, I killed a man on a bicycle. I ran from the scene. A half hour later, I dialed 911 and turned myself in.

I had skipped work that day and started drinking in the early afternoon. At about 6:30 that evening, I left a friend's house and began my six-mile journey home. The accident happened so fast I had no time to react.

I have been incarcerated for vehicular homicide since that night. Until then—despite three drunken driving citations in 11 years—I refused to admit that I had a problem with drinking. Those previous citations added six years to my prison sentence for killing the man whom I will call John.

The night of the accident, I swore I would never drink again. But after a year or so of being locked up, I changed it and said I will never drink and drive again.

Two years later, I received a letter from John's brother. He said he wasn't angry with me, and he forgave me, but he wanted my perspective on what had happened that night. Not a day went by without me thinking about the accident, but writing about it made me think even more about my actions on that day. After writing the letter, I knew I had to change, but I didn't know how. My counselor had suggested AA, but I refused to go.

While lying on my bunk one Friday evening, I heard the announcement for the AA meeting. I jumped up and went. Halfway through the Preamble, I realized that the date—February 20, 2004—was exactly three years since the accident. I took this as a sign and have been active in AA and practicing the Twelve Steps ever since.

After a year in the program—and four years after the accident—I wrote another letter to John's brother. I told him I belong to AA and practice the Twelve Steps in my life. I said I hoped my story might reach another alcoholic, and—in John's memory—save at least one family from the tragedy I had put his family through.

Ten months later, I received a miracle in the mail. This is the first page of an incredible letter I received from John's mother:

Dear James:

I am John's mother and will celebrate five years of sobriety on the 22nd of this month. I do not know what direction this letter will take—I leave it to God to guide me. Twenty-nine years ago I gave birth to John and, in honor of the way he lived and the loving memories I have of him, I find the right thing to do is to reach out to you. John's brother shared your letter of amends. I cannot describe the gratitude I felt and the healing that letter brought. I sobbed in my sponsor's arms and let go of so much of what I had kept inside me. Thank you. I pray that you will keep on the path of sobriety and receive God's love and forgiveness.

Her letter helped to lift a weight off me and strengthened my faith in the AA program. A Higher Power working in my life is the only explanation. Because of my faith and trust in a Higher Power, in my sponsor and in working the Twelve Steps, I have, for today, closed the door on my drinking as I try to carry the message of recovery and practice these principles in all my affairs.

James B.
Forks, Washington

Zipped Up Tight
September 2016

I was a salty newcomer, swaddled in my hoodie and leather jacket, not wanting to talk to anyone. That jacket had protected me everywhere, from sleeping behind dumpsters to traveling by freight train. Now I kept it zipped tight in the meeting that was to become my home group. I was a sexual assault survivor, and part of how I dealt with that was dressing so that many people mistook me for a young man. I kept my hair buzzed short.

After a month or so of listening in meetings, it began to dawn on me that AA people meant what they said. People weren't being nice because they expected something in return. It wasn't until much later that I understood this selflessness as the core of Step Twelve, and the foundation of the program.

Discovering AA was like experiencing a Christmas morning that wasn't going to end in a fight. I realized that the essential goodness in my heart, which I'd buried under crusty layers of beer coasters and cigarette butts, did not make me a chump. That goodness was being excavated, validated and reflected back to me by other folks in recovery.

My emotions started softening. I began to let my hair grow and started to wear makeup. I was scared. I felt more like my genuine self, but I wasn't used to male attention. I felt like a pubescent girl all over again.

Just the same, I softened quickly. I became very open. Some old-timers told me to stick with the women but my drinking buddies had been almost exclusively male. I didn't know how to talk to girls. I was intimidated by them. That's how I crossed paths with what I now recognize as a "13th stepper" on the prowl.

He was a bit older than me. I'll call him Glen. He worked at a rehab program and went to my home group. He always brought over a mob of dudes from the residence. They all sat together in their button-downs, sometimes looking shifty or haggard, but always freshly scrubbed. I found their disciplined appearance and cheery, irreverent manner appealing.

At the time, I wasn't in a rehab program. I still lived in a sort of crash-pad house with seven other young people who were all still drinking and using.

At AA meetings, Glen always talked to me, offering recovery advice or compliments. Once he rolled up on me in his truck as I was walking back home after a meeting. He offered me a ride. I don't remember what we talked about, but I clicked into flirtation mode, an old habit from hitchhiking, to get a ride as far as I could, maybe money, drugs or booze, and all while assessing the need for an exit strategy.

The next time I was in a meeting with Glen, he was beside me in the closing prayer circle. He rubbed my hand and caressed it instead of just holding it. I wanted to break away but felt I couldn't interrupt. I also felt that there was no way I could hold him responsible. No one would believe me if I said he had acted inappropriately.

I took a risk and broke my silence to a woman with more time than me. She assured me I wasn't the first person in AA to experience this. Talking to her gave me the courage to take action. I called Glen out on the group level in a meeting. I described his behavior without using his name. I told them he made me feel angry. The next person who spoke was a man. He said it wasn't appropriate to bring it up on group level. He said I was engaging in crosstalk.

I felt mortified, but the woman I'd confided in spoke next. She backed me up, saying that newcomers are vulnerable. She looked right at Glen and said this sort of thing happens too often.

Following the meeting, to my surprise, other women came up to me and thanked me for what I'd said. Shortly after that, I braved my first women's meeting and said I needed a sponsor. The woman who would become my sponsor came up to me afterward and asked if I was willing to go to any length to stay sober. I told her I was willing and we started to work the Steps. Glen left me alone after that meeting.

When my sponsor and I got to the Fourth Step, I still felt resentment toward Glen and a lot of other people. I had trouble seeing my part in the resentment. After all, I was the one who had been wronged. But my sponsor showed me that I had used Glen by taking rides from him when I disliked him. I came to understand this as a character defect, a survival tactic. It was one way I had kept my addiction fed. But it no longer served me.

When I got to Step Eight, Glen went on my amends list, even though I had misgivings. But with my sponsor's guidance, I understood that owning up to my part was about my growth and healing. It had nothing to do with whether he had done right or wrong. It had nothing to do with excusing or accepting his behavior.

With this understanding, I somehow had enough humility to make amends to him discreetly after a meeting. To my surprise, he apologized right back to me. Months later, in another meeting, I listened to him and heard his suffering. I was able to understand that, while he had acted that way to a newcomer, he was working through his own difficulties.

Making amends to Glen was an important lesson. It allowed me to move on and make amends to loved ones who my resentment would have blocked me from ever reconciling with. I had so much justified anger against them. But I had learned that I needed to heal myself and focus on my recovery. I am still close with the woman who backed me up in that meeting. She is one of my best friends in sobriety and I know she will get things that I can't talk even to my sponsor about.

I wore my leather jacket to a concert the other night, without fear of drinking, but most of the time it hangs in my closet. I don't need it to sleep safely or to hide my emotions anymore. Today I wear my heart on my sleeve.

Anonymous

Spiritual Agony
February 2001

Making an amends to the murderer of a precious friend was the most terrifying prospect—next to taking another drink—that I have faced in sobriety. But it also turned out to be the most liberating action I have ever taken sober and the opportunity for which I am most grateful.

My drinking career was short but intense, complete with downing eye-openers on hangover mornings, innumerable blackouts (including a few of the four-day-long, wake-up-in-another-country variety), two car accidents, and four stints in the psych ward, where I detoxed for what I pray was the last time. I was 19 years old.

I have been sober now for almost two years, and I never cease to be amazed at how deeply the Promises come true for me as I incorporate the principles of our program into my life. However, the first six months of sobriety were enormously painful. I got little relief from the spiritual agony I was in, and because I did not take the Steps, my compulsion to drink was not lifted.

One chilly October night, as I waited for a ride, shivering and half-heartedly participating in an after-the-meeting meeting, someone suggested that I pray the Third Step prayer and get to work on a Fourth Step. To put it mildly, I balked. I had read the Big Book and sat in enough meetings to know that taking inventory of my resentments—and forgiving those who had wronged me—would play large roles in working the Fourth and Fifth Steps. But because I was, in my mind, the epitome of an innocent victim, I saw no reason to forgive anyone, and I nursed my resentments as if my life depended upon keeping them alive.

Finally I had had enough. My spiritual agony was becoming unbearable. I didn't want to drink again, and without fail, every AA I met with a quality of sobriety I wanted had taken the Fourth and Fifth Steps thoroughly. As one of them put it: "If you want what I have, do what I do." So I sat down and wrote my Fourth Step.

Then in admitting my wrongs to another human being, I was able to see that my resentments had not just been eating my lunch; they had been ruling my life. The people for whom I burned with hatred didn't even know I hated them, and if they did, they probably wouldn't care. My anger was poisoning my soul, not theirs. I wanted to hurt them and was only hurting myself. It was as if I were swallowing rat poison and waiting for those I thought were rats to die. And I was truly surprised that it didn't work.

One especially difficult resentment was a reasonably justified one. When I was a teenager, a dear friend was murdered. He had been an important part of my life and the closest thing I had to a father. When he died, I felt as if I had been dropped into a shark tank with an anvil tied to my foot. "Swim!" the whole world seemed to be saying, jeering at my confusion, loss and pain.

His killer was found guilty but insane, and sent to a state mental institution. Imagining the murderer in a paint-chipped ward full of drooling patients in straitjackets gave me some relief. At least she was locked up and in a terrible place, although that wasn't bad enough, of course. The only fitting justice for her was to be slowly tortured to death with my bare hands. And not even that would have satisfied me. I wanted the killer to hurt like I was hurting, and that just wasn't possible.

In the rooms of AA, I found a God of my own understanding, and with his help, I was able to forgive the person who had caused me this deep pain. But forgiving is not forgetting, and the death of my friend occupied a lot of space in my mind and heart on a daily basis. Though I no longer burned with hatred, the killer was still living in my head rent-free.

I prayed for compassion and received it. One night I was struck with the realization of how lucky I am. All the mistakes I made when I was ill had been repaired to the best of my ability; none of them had been permanent and final. The agony of being responsible for someone else's death is a horrible thing. I learned that in the rooms of AA while listening to people whose drinking led to another's death, usually when they were behind the wheel of a car. There but for the grace of God went I. As an active alcoholic, I was a potential killer every day. That was the truth, and like all truth, it was hard to swallow. I also realized that when my friend's killer was restored to sanity through proper medication for her mental illness, an overwhelming and unamendable regret would be part of her life forever.

A few days after reaching 18 months of sobriety, I knew that the time had come for me, with God's help, to do my best to set the situation right. I had learned in AA the power of forgiveness and the freedom it offers, both in being forgiven and extending it to others. I wanted that freedom.

My friend was dead; I could not change that. What I could do was make amends for selfishly nursing my resentment. I had burned much energy in useless anger and hatred, and the best way to set that right would be to do what I could to promote healing.

Taking a friend with more than a decade of sobriety, I went to visit the killer in the mental institution. I was clumsy and fumbled my words, but what came out was what was truly in my sober heart: "The person you killed was like a father to me. He meant the world to me. I loved him more than I can put into words. But I have come to a place where it's OK. I used to hate you for taking him away from me, but I don't anymore. I forgive you completely, I sincerely wish you all the best in your life, and I hope you keep getting better. I knew it would be good for me to come here to tell you that, and I hope it will help you to know that someone who loved him very much and was affected really hard by losing him has moved on and forgives you and it's OK."

Grateful that my voice didn't crack and that I didn't get sick from the butterflies dancing in my stomach, I took a deep breath and said a silent prayer of thanks. Then I sat and watched as the human being in front of me expressed the most sincere sorrow and regret I have ever seen. It allowed me to make peace with my loss. Now I believe that mental illness had robbed this woman of the power of choice, and my friend had died because he was just in a bad place at a bad time.

As I walked down the sidewalk back to my car, I felt the deepest level of forgiveness I've ever known. A 500-pound weight was lifted from my shoulders. I felt free and cleansed. I had just found wings, and they were mine.

Holly H.
Huntsville, Alabama

CHAPTER SEVEN

Active Alcoholism and Money: An Amends Waiting to Happen

———◇———

A brave reconciliation with our financial failures is an investment like no other

I n the following story, "9th Step Ride," Scotty K. quotes a memorable AA speaker who said: "It's amazing how for a little money we often sell out our happiness." The writer, like so many, had always avoided making money amends. But a stubbornly lingering unhappiness drives him to take the difficult step that gives him peace when all others failed.

Steve H. describes his financial liberation in the article "On the Other Side of Amends," addressing the hesitant by noting that their unfinished business, "will eat at them until they square it with that person, like a dripping faucet in their mind and heart."

Karen P.'s sponsor thought it unnecessary that she pay back a rehab she had stolen from. But Karen knew better, and the rehab director suggested she bring in much-needed meetings to the residents. In "If It Ain't Nailed Down," Karen exults in her new freedom from the thievery that had haunted her. "Now ... I remember the kids and the meetings and the service—not the stolen goods in my trunk."

Sometimes it's not just about the money. Doug R., in the story "Bank Notes," describes paying his dad back every Friday, always including a chatty note. At his dad's death, Doug discovered his father had lovingly saved every one.

And Ross K, in the story "Right to the Edge," admits he's an embezzler doing time for his crime. But having made a difficult amends to *his former employer, he speaks for all on the other side of the bars as he writes, "When I am released, I will be six years sober, a free man with no baggage or secrets."*

9th Step Ride
September 2008

I n early sobriety an old-timer whom I admired once said to me, "Scotty, one day you're gonna have to do these Steps for real!"

That day came at five years of sobriety. At that time I seemed to be getting sicker. It wasn't really that my habits had changed. It was that my head had, and I couldn't stand the way I was anymore. It's been said that while many people make it to five years of sobriety, the numbers drop off significantly after that. This statistic made me nervous. I tried more meetings, but that didn't seem to work. Something had to give.

So I got in touch with a guy I knew from a men's Step study. I went to him and said, "OK, what do I do now?" He responded by handing me a Big Book before sending me off with much reading and writing to do. So I did what he said and then returned for a new assignment. It was like taking a class in college, then doing the homework. The end result was that I rather quickly became somebody I really liked, somebody really cool.

Eventually though, my involvement in AA beyond meeting attendance tapered off and I began to rest on my laurels. By six-and-a-half years of sobriety, I was again in emotional pain.

It was summertime and I was about to embark on one of my cross-country, multiple-month motorcycle rides. The open highway, a good running bike, a sunny day, no time limits and a few bucks to spare—my personal idea of nirvana. I could hardly wait!

And so the day came when I hit the road with extra clothes stuffed into the saddlebags, a tent and sleeping bag strapped behind. But inside, I still hurt. The pain, it seemed, was following.

I headed for a place I'd been to many times before, a place I knew I'd be happy: Serenity Run, a small, sober motorcycle rally located in

Colorado. The rally was good and the friendship even better, but the pain persisted.

But there was good news on the horizon, for after the Serenity Run, I would move on to the Sturgis Rally in South Dakota. This was one I'd attended many times before, and always had a good time. The event went great. I saw old friends, picked up a few concerts, did my fair share of dancing and attended many AA meetings. But it was not enough, for the pain was not diminished and again my fun was mostly feigned.

My next plan was to ride out and visit an old girlfriend who lived in Minnesota. That would fix it for sure! But it only made things worse. And so I rode on.

Eventually I found myself holed up in a cheap hotel in Billings, Montana. The weather had turned cold now and, knowing no one in that fair city, isolation mounted into ever-deepening despair. Desperation. It thickened.

For some reason, the Ninth Step came to mind. I'd done some Ninth Step amends before, but had carefully avoided any that had to do with money. Being the self-centered tightwad I am, I'd determined that those were the amends I didn't have to make. But my growing desperation soon spawned a new willingness and with it a decision was made. First, I'd ride south and into warmer weather again (motorcycle riders will understand the wisdom of this decision). Second, I'd return to my little hometown in the mountains of southern California—the place I'd done most of my drinking—and give some money to the landlord I'd run out on over six-and-a-half years before. His name was on my list of amends and I owed him $500. I figured I'd offer him $250 as a start. The idea already made me mad. But it didn't really matter, I reasoned, since I wasn't having too much fun anyway.

The further south I went, the warmer it got, and I sat shirtless as the big Harley made its way across the open desert. In a state of semi-insanity by now, I started talking out loud to God about the forthcoming errand. "You know, Big Guy," I said, "I'm not going up there to do this thing because I'm such a nice guy, or even 'cause I'm such a spiritual human being. Truth is, I'm going up here to buy 250 bucks worth of serenity!" At that point I laughed like a drunken hyena. With all other avenues exhausted, desperation was driving me to actual Step work.

Upon arrival, I parked the bike in a space in front of the small office of my former landlord. In a moment, his van pulled into the slot beside my own and he stepped out of the car. "Arthur," I said. "Remember me?" He squinted. "No."

Being a low-bottom drunk, I guessed my appearance must have changed some in the intervening six-and-a-half years, so I reminded him. "Oh ... yeah," he mumbled, as recognition dawned. Arthur did not look happy to see me. But he'd always been a nice guy. And even through it all, I'd liked him.

"Can I come in and talk for a moment?"

Once seated in the little office, I quickly ran through my pitch. I'd been studying the Ninth Step instructions contained in the little Big Book carried aboard my bike. As instructed there, I spoke briefly of my alcoholism, then emphasized my wish to set right any wrongs I'd done him in the past. "I can offer you $250 now, then pay the rest when possible. Will that be all right?" It was.

When the time came to go, I reached for his hand, but the man surprised me with a big bear hug instead.

So I left Arthur and was soon on the way home to San Diego. As the road opened up ahead of me, my thoughts wandered off to romance and a girl I knew back home who might be able to help fix my problem. Then it hit me: it was a beautiful day, I was doing something I truly loved ... and I felt just fine. The pain was gone, replaced by contentment and happiness! I was shocked. An AA talk I'd heard came to mind. "It's amazing," the speaker had said of the Ninth Step, "how for a little money we often sell out our happiness." It was true. Why making this amend had worked when all else had failed, I knew not—and still don't. It just did. And that was good enough.

Within a few months, I'd finished my financial obligation to Arthur. I've run into him on occasion in the years since and we are friends. It took longer to pay the others, but I eventually attended to those, too.

Although sobriety is not always easy, its payoff has often far surpassed whatever dreams I thought I had. We all have the opportunity to go out and take our shot at this life. We become mothers and fathers. Sons and daughters. Families. We buy houses. Attend school. Change, or gain, careers. Become business owners. Get married. Get divorced. Take vacations to Hawaii. Outfit boats and sail around the world. Coach Little League. Travel by motorcycle. The list of things to do and love in this world is endless.

The disease took my shot at life away. AA gave it back.

Scotty K.
Lake Arrowhead, California

Right to the Edge
April 2006

M y name is Ross R., and I am 41 years old. I am currently serving an 18 month sentence in a federal prison, a sentence that resulted from making my Ninth Step amends.

I came to AA on February 28, 1999, and have been sober ever since. A thorough Ninth Step and willingness to do anything my sponsor asked has helped me remain sober.

On January 2, 2000, when I was 11 months sober, my sponsor, Olaf G., and I went hiking in the Hollywood Hills. We discussed my Ninth Step; I knew he would bring up the one amend I had not made. For seven years, I had embezzled quite a large amount of money from an employer. I quit that job in my third month of sobriety because I could not stop stealing. My sponsor told me that he had discussed my situation with many old-timers and had been directed to the Big Book for the answer.

I had no family to support, my sponsor said, and following his direction would not harm others. He advised me to turn myself in to that company and make amends.

I wish I could say I followed his directions without question right away, but I told him no. He gave me two weeks to decide. In the meantime, he asked that I read the Big Book and pray. I said I would.

I took the two weeks, but I knew that I really had no choice. I wanted the Promises that are promised to each of us. I needed this lifted from my shoulders, or I would drink again.

On January 12, 2000, I went to my former employer and made my amends. What started out as one of my worst days—because I was so scared—became one of my best days when it was over. Because I had trusted God, my sponsor and AA, that trinity had lifted the weight that was on my shoulders for so long. I felt sober.

What I thought would be a quick process turned into three and a half years of waiting. In March 2003, federal government representatives came to my apartment and presented me with a plea agreement that would place me in prison for anywhere from 18 months to five years.

Once again, I fell back in the arms of AA. Fortunately, I had kept going to meetings and had a sponsor, so I had a support network helping me during that time. I found a lawyer in the program; she walked me through this process with incredible dignity and grace. I started sharing at any meeting I could, trying to find people with an experience similar to this. I would be lying if I said I didn't go through many days resenting the amends, and feeling alone in my process. My sponsor and support group helped me realize that I am not alone, and my experience would one day help someone else.

The day of sentencing came. I cannot describe how overwhelming that is to experience. Your future held in the hands of others, and an overwhelming regret that past behavior has brought you to this point. I shared these feelings at meetings. On sentencing day, AA packed the courthouse with over 70 fellow AAs showing their support. That awful day turned into one of great meaning and we felt a spiritual experience in that courtroom.

The judge said she had never seen such a large turnout for anyone in all her years on the bench. Prosecutors recommended the minimum sentence and I was sentenced to 18 months in federal prison.

My sponsor and an AA buddy took me in to surrender on the day ordered, and will be there to pick me up on the day I get out, as long as we all stay sober.

I spent the first eight days in a maximum-security prison and I can say they were the worst days of my life. I was angry with God and with AA, and felt abandoned by both. On the seventh day, I got on my knees and prayed to God, saying that I had enough and could not go on anymore. They moved me the next morning to where I am today and, once again, I was reminded that God never gives me more than I can handle, but sometimes he takes me right to the edge.

When I am released, I will be six years sober, a free man with no baggage or secrets. AA will be there for me, and I will be there for it. If I can spend the rest of my life helping others in the walk of sobriety, then I will have a good life.

Ross R.
Taft, California

On the Other Side of Amends
Grapevine Online Exclusive
May 2011

The Steps can take unexpected twists. When it comes to making right past mistakes and harms, also known as Step Nine, my experience has been my making amends to others. But this story is about being on the receiving end of someone making an amends to me.

About five years ago, I had a guy working for me who was very likable, fairly good at his work, and had the greatest stories about why he would be late or unable to work. For instance, one time he developed Crohn's disease and couldn't come to work because he was at the hospital the night before. Another time he was going to be late for work because he ran into the front of a garbage truck. And yet another time a tire on his car came off while he was driving to work. Not so surprisingly, his drinking and drug use was growing all the time while he worked for me.

At the end of our working relationship, I agreed to pay him in advance for a few hours of work he was going to do for me over the weekend. And, you guessed it, he never showed. In fact, he plain disappeared, moved out of state. I don't remember getting a grudge toward him over this, but I do remember being somewhat disappointed and amused with myself for falling for his con.

With time and prayer, plus guidance from the Big Book chapter "To Employers," where it talks about forgiving employees who mistreat the boss because of their sickness, I let go of the whole situation and eventually laughed at the irony of how I used to treat employers the same way.

Fast forward to about a year ago, and out of the blue the same guy calls me from another city basically confessing his addiction and how sorry he is for treating me the way he did and how he is in recovery and would like to repay me the money he felt he owed me. I laughed and agreed to let him repay me and gave him my address. Well, good thing I didn't buy something expecting to have his money pay for it.

So a couple of months ago he started calling again, saying he was most likely going to move back to Boise and he would like to get together and yes, make good on what he owed me by working off his debt. I told him to forget about it, but he insisted it was something he must do. I understood. As I write, he's scheduled to work for me next week—on credit. The funny thing about it is that the wage I can pay him is about 35 percent less than it was five years ago, so he's going to have to work more to make right his wrong. Moreover, it has been suggested to me to pay him for his effort and go through the ritual of letting him give me the money he owes; a true closing of the deal.

In the end, it's interesting to see how unfinished business in someone who is trying to live right by spiritual principles will eat at them until they square it with that person, like a dripping faucet in their mind and heart. It is also a blessing for me to have been able to forgive him for what is now a matter of no issue and to allow him the opportunity to be set free from his past. Well, stay tuned, he hasn't actually worked for me yet.

Steve H.

Tax Returns
September 2008

I was just a few days past my 50th birthday when God gave me another opportunity to escape from alcoholism. I was introduced to AA through an angelic telephone operator who directed me to the late Scotty A., an alcoholism treatment worker. From day one, AA fit me like a tailor-made suit because willingness to listen and learn was included in God's initial package of grace for me. Those qualities are still with me over 20 years later. Within a very short time after my first meeting, I wanted everything AA had to offer.

During some 35 years of progressive alcoholism, I became a proficient user of people, businesses and the system. By the time I sobered up, I had a pile of bad debts and legal instruments registered against me. The asset side of my ledger might as well have been totally blank. I had defrauded a supplier to my small construction business and could certainly have been charged and convicted. Instead, soon after sobering up, I took responsibility for the debt and started paying it off monthly. I made those payments for years. In addition, I had somehow managed to go 23 years without filing a personal income tax return. How resolution of that situation played out became a lasting, strong spiritual lesson, namely that God brings his influence to bear at the most unusual times and in the most unusual places. That is the point of this story.

When I got to Step Eight, I knew that my amends to the taxman had to be made, in part because cheating the taxman was a corrosive form of self-dishonesty. For me, self-honesty had become an essential character trait. Perfection? No. But I had to give it my best shot.

By my third year of sobriety, most of my debts had been taken care of or were in the process of being paid off. I frequently contemplated how I would satisfy the taxman, who represented my last and biggest unresolved debt. Then one day the taxman came to me, in the form of a phone call from a collections officer with Revenue Canada. Let's call her Helen. She was pleasant but firm, and obviously well-trained and experienced. She was only interested in how and when I would pay what Revenue Canada said I owed. No, they were not interested in negotiating the amount owed. And no, monthly payments were not an option. I was fully at the mercy of the taxman. The agenda was definitely now all hers. I said I needed time.

Helen called again in two weeks to see if I now had the wherewithal to pay my debt. I said I needed more time, but that I would pay in full as soon as I could. I admitted I was a recovering alcoholic and explained that the AA program strongly encouraged me to take full responsibility for my checkered past and set things right. She said she understood. However, she would soon need a firm payment date.

Two weeks later Helen called again. This time she asked if I was planning to attend an AA roundup in her city. She was on the organizing committee and had some eight years of sobriety. To say that I was surprised would be a huge understatement. We talked about the AA program for a few minutes. It was a mini-meeting on the telephone. Her disclosure that she was also in AA did not reduce the magnitude of my financial plight, but it did make it seem more manageable and human, and therefore more palatable. She said I would have to borrow money from whatever sources I could find because I was running out of time. The deadline to pay, before I would be facing possible legal conviction for tax evasion, was nearing. The potential consequences of my pre-sobriety behavior tested my ability to accept life on life's terms. Helen agreed to a further extension of two weeks. I think that came out of her personal generosity toward a fellow alcoholic and AA member.

The local bank said no again to my loan application, because it was not yet seven years since I had cleared up a legal judgment against me.

My wife was full of anxiety, afraid that we would find no source of money. But I had come to accept that life would unfold the way it wants to. My job was to accept life's decisions and respond appropriately.

We went to the only other financial institution in town and sat down with the branch manager, whose name I knew, but who was a stranger to me. I explained my predicament, laying it out with all my newfound self-honesty. He asked for my signature on a promissory note. Then he instructed me to open an account on my way out and he would deposit in it what I needed to pay the taxman. I was flabbergasted. Had he just agreed to lend me some money—or, in fact, all the money I needed for the taxman? He saw the puzzled look in my eyes. Indeed, he was lending me the full debt amount. He said that he knew of my length of sobriety and my involvement in AA, and that the community considered me a citizen in good standing. He explained that his brother was at that time sober nine years, thanks to Alcoholics Anonymous. He believed that I would stay sober and pay the loan back in full. I think he approved the loan for me as his way of thanking AA for saving his brother's life.

My wife and I could barely wait to get home and phone Helen. She suggested we come to her city and her office to conclude this matter. Although we had never met face-to-face before, I walked into her glass-walled office and we embraced, smiled a lot, and talked about AA for some time. I paid my income tax debt in full and we had a long hug again before I left. I doubt that her coworkers had ever seen a collections officer hug a tax delinquent before.

There are those who would call these events a fortuitous string of coincidences. I believe it is the very obvious work of a Higher Power. The instant bond between three strangers—alcoholic, taxman, and money lender—was deeply human, woven with compassion, honesty and the utmost respect for one another. It was, therefore, spiritual. In my experience, spiritual interactions between humans are often the silent work of a Higher Power.

Anonymous
Saskatchewan

From At Wit's End
November 2008

A new AA was having trouble sleeping because he felt guilty for cheating on his income taxes. His sponsor suggested he make amends, so he sent the IRS the following letter:

> *Dear Sir or Madam:*
> *I cheated on my taxes and cannot sleep until I make amends.*
> *Enclosed is a check for $500.*
> *Sincerely,*
> *A reformed citizen*
> *P.S. If I still can't sleep, I'll send you the balance.*
>
> Bud B.
Satellite Beach, Florida

Hot Wine
March 2013

One spring day my AA friend Ray P. and I were taking a side trip from the North Coast AA Roundup in Seaside, Oregon. Panning for gold was one of Ray's hobbies, so we were heading down south to Tillamook to check out a sluice Ray was interested in. I was along for the ride to see some of the beautiful Oregon coast.

My aunt and uncle had lived in Tillamook. I grew up in Seaside. This was my old stomping ground, and I wanted to see it again. I tried not to bore Ray to death with stories of the past, including the many memories of the last days of my drinking. But I never want to completely forget those days of suicidal thought and "incomprehensible demoralization." That was more than 20 years ago.

On the way in the car, a memory returned to me in a powerful way. I remembered coming back from Tillamook once, when I pulled into the parking lot of a small winery. There was no one around, but I saw a pallet of wine. I got out of my old battered car, walked around the stack of wine, and decided to steal a case. I grabbed one, threw it in my back seat and drove off. I told Ray about this incident in my past and said, "There is an amend I need to make."

Sometime later that day, I decided I had better follow through and make the amend, so I wrote the following email:

> To whom it may concern at the winery:
>
> Around 1976, I stopped at your winery on my way back from Tillamook to Seaside. I was drinking alcoholically during those days. There was a pallet of wine sitting there, and I stole a case. This past April I was in Seaside for the North Coast AA Roundup, and my friend Ray and I drove to Tillamook. I remembered the time I stole the case of wine. It is part of my recovery in AA to make amends for the wrong and selfish things I did then.

I then told him the name of the wine I stole and asked him how much it would cost, and that I would send him a check for that amount. A man, also named Ray, emailed me back:

> Michael, wow, that was a surprise. Just to let you know, that was the first time something like this has happened. I have been wondering whether to charge you or to give you the case as a reward for the wonderful change in your life. Back then, a case of that particular wine sold for $72; now it sells for $240. If we calculate the current value of the $72 at only 6% interest compounded, it's about $519. If you want, please take a look at our webpage and look at the links to the newspaper article about our projects in Cambodia. We have started an orphanage in Cambodia and several other projects to help that country's poor. Whatever it is you can pay, 100% could go to the

orphanage and schools. Any amount will be very helpful. Michael, if you are strapped, do not send money just now. But please continue to help others and let them know about your progress. Thank so much for this wonderful bright spot in my life. The universe loves us all.

Thank you, Ray

I was flush, so I decided to send the $240. I made two $60 payments and one $120 payment over the next few months. Ray then sent me a contribution receipt from his foundation, with a handwritten note, which said:

Michael, thank you so much for your actions; they are truly unusual and restore my faith in our country and its people.

Thanks, Ray

Once again the fruits of the Ninth Step were beyond my dreams. This incident reminded me how AA works. My selfish and wrong deeds from my drinking days were transformed into a gift to poor families in Cambodia. Only God, if we follow his way in spite of our contrary thoughts, can turn stolen wine into a source of renewal for two men and benefits to people in need.

Michael P.
Puyallup, Washington

If It Ain't Nailed Down
March 2013

While my drinking career only spanned five years, my alcoholic behavior had been such that I had a really long list of people to whom I owed amends. At first I felt really hopeless about it. I thought I'd made such a mess of my life that it couldn't possibly be fixed. Still, I began the process of making those amends, starting with my family first and then working through my list. Each amend I made gave me a little more hope that perhaps my life could change.

My sponsor helped me sort through which of the amends I needed to make directly, and which ones would be harmful to others. She also steered me away from making amends for things when she didn't think I'd done anything wrong. One that she claimed I didn't need to make was to the adolescent treatment center in which I'd found sobriety. I felt horribly guilty because when I left, I took a lot of things from the facility. I stole small things, like books, but bigger things too, like a lamp and a comforter, and pretty much anything that I liked that wasn't nailed down. Besides, the facility was closing, and I thought it was better to take the stuff for someone who could use it (me!) than to leave it for the parent corporation to reallocate to other facilities. A disgruntled employee had actually helped me load the goods into my car.

My sponsor reasoned that if the facility was closing at the time of my departure, it wasn't really stealing. I felt guilty, though, because the facility ended up reopening a few months later. My sponsor kept telling me that I needed to just let this one go, but it didn't feel right. I was certainly living my life differently, but despite my sponsor's view of the situation, I couldn't just let it go. I finally told her that I was going to make amends anyway, and I called the facility to ask what their needs were. I wasn't financially in a position to make a huge monetary amend, but I figured I could start by buying them some bedding or donating some clothes for the residents who sometimes arrive with only the clothes on their backs.

The woman who answered the phone had worked there when I was a resident and was delighted to hear from me. She was happy to hear that I was still sober and doing well. I told her why I was calling—what I had done years before and what I wanted to do about it. She told me that they didn't need goods, but they did need volunteers. It seemed that a small group of local AA members that had been bringing meetings into the center had stopped coming, and since the facility was a lockdown, that meant the residents no longer got to go to any AA meetings at all. She asked me if I'd be willing to talk to my AA friends and bring in regular meetings.

At first, this seemed like too much of a request. I lived almost two hours away. And while I was connected to AA in my local community, I didn't know many people in the district where the treatment center was located. But I talked to some of my local connections, particularly other young people, and found several members who really wanted to do this. So I committed to doing it with them, and we started a Saturday night meeting in the facility.

Sometimes we'd go early and have dinner with the residents, and we'd almost always stay after and hang out. It was a great commitment and a wonderful way for me to make a living amend. I kept this commitment until I moved out of the area.

The best part of making this amend is that now, when I think of the facility, I don't feel guilty at all. I remember the kids and the meetings and the service—not the stolen goods in my trunk.

Karen P.
Franklin, New Hampshire

Bank Notes
September 1999

When I was two years sober, I decided it was time to make some financial amends to my father. He had loaned me a lot of money through my years of drinking to cover rent, child support, etc. I figured it must be $2,000 or $3,000. I said to my dad, "I owe you some money and I want to pay you back."

"Don't worry about that money," he said. "I don't need it. I'm just happy you've got your life back on track. Forget about it."

I said, "No, I have to do this—it's one of those damned Steps. This is something I have to do to stay sober. Do you know how much I owe you?" "No," said my dad, "but I've got it in the computer." (He didn't need it, but he did save it!)

He sent me a printout of the loans, which added up to around

$7,200. I was surprised; I guess I had kind of lost track. I started sending him a check every Friday. Sometimes a little, sometimes a lot—whatever I could afford that week. And because this was my dad, and not some faceless creditor, I also included a little note. Just a short note saying what I was up to that week or sometimes a joke or something jotted down on a Post-It or a steno sheet.

After about three years, he called to say that I had dwindled the debt down to $32. I sent him the $32 and he returned a "closeout notice." The debt was paid in full. The only thing my father had to say about it was, "I'm gonna miss those notes."

It turned out there was a benefit I never expected. Always in the past, when I would go out to dinner with him, he would insist on picking up the check. I'd become very irritated. "Hey, I'm a grown man. Let me get the check once in a while. Let me take my father out to dinner."

"I'm the father here. I'll get it," he would say.

But after that debt was settled, I had no problem allowing him to get the check. Once I was no longer in his debt (financially) I could allow him to be the father, to buy dinner for his kid. Sometimes we don't recognize the baggage we're carrying until it's gone.

My dad developed cancer a few years back and it finally took him in 1997. After his death, I was going through some of his papers with my mother. I came across a file with my name on it. When I opened it, I discovered all the notes I had sent him with the checks. There were about 150 of them. I was stunned. I said to my mom, "Did you know about this?"

"Yeah," she smiled, "I said to him one time, 'Doug sure loves you,' and he said, 'I know that—I've got it in his own handwriting.'"

That's one of the gifts I received from the Steps. My sponsor never told me about that one. How could he have known?

Doug R.
Tujunga, California

CHAPTER EIGHT

Finally Reaching Out to Those We So Often Kept at Bay

———◇———

Our friends and coworkers, who were always
close at hand, easy targets for our addictive behavior,
are now recipients of our amends

How often did we isolate from and abandon our friends, or leave our work for others to do when we were absentees, sickened by our addiction? With Step Nine it's possible to have a richer life lived fully in the present, accompanied by a cast of untroubled characters.

In this chapter's story "A Reminder at the Reunion," an intimate four-woman, 50-year high school gathering in Maine was the opportunity for writer Joan L. to respond to one shy classmate's whispered admission: "I felt bullied then, too." A prayerful time in her room enabled Joan to make an equally quiet and honest amend to her old friend for her part in that hurtful behavior.

Alcoholic paranoia about a successful woman coworker from Hong Kong led the anonymous writer of "Letter to Hong Kong," to humiliate her in front of their colleagues. Much later, sober, she wrote down her amends and, "As I heard the squeaky slamming of the mailbox," she remembers, "a great burden began to lift from me ... the fate of my letter remains unknown. But the gift it bestowed on me is forever certain."

In "A Letter from an Old Friend," Dave B. had not corresponded for 20 years with a once dear long-time friend, the first person to suggest he had a problem with alcohol. Dave was sober four years when he *finally found and wrote to her. She answered his letter graciously, telling him that her husband had committed suicide, most likely prompted by alcoholic depression, and marveled at the epiphany that saved Dave from that fate.*

A drinking buddy, Zeke, got writer James L. fired for his bad behavior on the job in the story "Digging Out." When James got sober he knew an amends was in order, but he had no plans to look up a guy who could be so mean. So guess who showed up at James's AA meeting looking for a temporary sponsor?

Among the old friends and coworkers who witnessed our destructive behavior at close range are brand new relationships just waiting for the healing power of Step Nine.

A Reminder at the Reunion
Grapevine Online Exclusive
August 2011

I was looking forward to a reunion with four women I had gone to high school with 50 years ago. Our weekends together had become an annual event. A stay in Maine in a lovely home surrounded by trees, flowers and blue sky was much anticipated. It was a time to come together to relive old memories and to make new ones. At times it felt like the pajama parties of the 1950s.

I was not overly concerned that they would be drinking wine. They knew of my sobriety and had been supportive. I had my literature and phone numbers. I looked forward to celebrating 35 years of sobriety in another month.

These were women who I drank with. My first experience of getting drunk happened with three of these women when we were 15. Barb (our hostess in Maine) had a babysitting job for a neighbor. She invited Lillian and me to keep her company. While Barb watched the children, Lillian and I had spotted the bottles of alcohol lining the family room wall and we decided to sample them. I felt like Alice in Wonderland with all these magic potions.

This was the first of my alcoholic drinking. For the next 18 years, I drank for effect. That was the beginning of blackout drinking, the loss of the values I had been taught, the mental obsession around alcohol and the physical compulsion after the first drink. Barb lost her job because of this, I had a hangover and a blackout, and yet I looked forward to when I could do this again! My disease progressed until my life spiraled out of control. Soon after, I arrived in Alcoholics Anonymous. I was 33 years old.

On Saturday evening, we started reminiscing about one of our classmates who was now deceased. We had bullied and teased her unmercifully. My friends chalked this up to adolescent behavior but I disagreed because I was ashamed of my part in this. As we discussed this, our hostess quietly announced that she felt she also was the target of our cruelty. This brought a hush over the room and she also announced she had forgiven us and that she loved us.

Later in my room, I thanked God for another day of sobriety. I then asked for guidance about making amends to my friend Barb for my part in destructive and hurtful behavior. I reflected that although I thought I had done the Eighth and Ninth Steps, I had not been very thorough. I had tended to see myself as the victim rather than see the harm I had done others.

The following day the chance came and I was able to give a heartfelt "I am so sorry for having hurt you." I was able to share with her some of my old feelings that I had back in high school: That I had never felt good enough or pretty enough, and that sobriety has given me an opportunity to become a woman of dignity and worth. I think we both experienced a sense of healing.

Joan L.
Gloucester, Massachusetts

Letter to Hong Kong
March 2013

When I went to do my Eighth Step, my anxiety mushroomed. Most of my amends would be relatively easy, but there was one in particular that made me as sick to my stomach as any hangover had. I had offended an innocent person profoundly and publicly. Not only did I slander and insult this person in front of others without justification, I never even attempted to apologize.

I was working at a large firm in San Francisco. Hours were long, and my nerves were jangled as I tried to climb the corporate ladder while "managing my stress" with heavy drinking after work each night. In those days, drinking at lunch was acceptable. Paranoia was my prevailing emotion, and I did not have the pedigree to be on partnership track at this firm. I occasionally produced high-quality work, but mostly it was very hungover quality. But I could get clients in the door. I had a knack for that.

We had a visiting professional from Hong Kong, an intelligent, soft-spoken woman who was about my age and experience level. Let's call her Lilly. Lilly was assigned to work on a couple of my clients' projects. The clients seemed to really like Lilly a lot. In fact, some of them started calling her directly.

Growing jealous, I made some effort to intimidate Lilly. I told her that we did things in the U.S. far differently than what she was used to, and one wrong step could get her (and the firm) into serious trouble.

My brooding over Lilly and her popularity at the firm and with my clients became more and more pronounced. I was starting to glare at her in the hallways and roll my eyes while she was speaking. Eventually, I was bad-mouthing her with others in the firm. Soon I could think of nothing else but Lilly.

One day I called in sick, which probably meant I was hungover. Around 8 P.M., it occurred to me that I should check my voicemail. There was a message from Lilly. She said she had been called in to see the CEO and board of directors about a deal. After hearing that, I stayed up all night stewing in my hatred, pouring shots and plotting revenge.

When morning came, I showered and brushed my teeth, trying to force the alcohol out of my pores and cells. I put makeup under my eyes to camouflage the dark circles and went into work to confront Lilly. I accused her of "trying to steal my client" and "back-stabbing" me. I told her she was unethical, a liar, a cheater and a desperate climber who couldn't get her own clients if her life depended on it. And that was the nice part. I concluded by telling her to go back to Hong Kong where apparently this is how "your kind" behaves. A number of co-workers heard my tirade. Lilly was in tears.

Lilly soon went back to Hong Kong. Eventually, I was nudged and then shoved out of that firm. Two years later, I found the rooms of AA. When it came time for Step Nine, I knew I would have to do something about Lilly. It was now four years later. There was no internet back then, and I only had Lilly's first and last names and the name of her law firm in Hong Kong. My sponsor thought it would upset Lilly if I were to call her. She would not want to hear my voice. But she might be willing to read a letter from me.

So I sat down and wrote a letter to her. I told her that the things I had said were horrible and untrue. I told her that my actions had been positively uncivilized and that she did not deserve any of it. I told her that I had deep regret and remorse and that I just wanted her to know that I was very sorry. I said that I wish her only wellness and happiness in her life.

I folded the letter and sealed it in the envelope addressed to Lilly at the Hong Kong firm, with a request to forward. As I heard the squeaky slamming of the mailbox, a great burden began to lift from me. I stood there on the sidewalk, suddenly transformed. I knew that I wanted to stay sober more than I had ever wanted anything in life. The fate of my letter remains unknown. But the gift it bestowed on me is forever certain.

Anonymous

Digging Out
March 2013

Zeke and I first met at a cabinet factory right after my Army discharge. He drove a tractor-trailer for them while I worked in the final assembly area and the loading dock. After I moved into the trailer park where he lived with his wife we began drinking together and generally enjoyed each other's company.

It did not take long to drink myself out of the job with the cabinet factory. Zeke was now working as a backhoe operator for a plumbing company, and he managed to get me hired there as an assistant ditch-digger.

My drinking and dietary habits at the time did not provide the strength needed for that kind of physical labor. I was listless and hungover on the job. I needed instructions for even the simplest tasks, even such plain jobs as, "Put up that shovel, put your foot on the blade, and move this dirt to that pile."

Finally, the owner of the company decided it wasn't safe to have me on site around the machinery. He fired me with Zeke's ready approval. Another job lost due to my incompetence, but I felt deeply betrayed. I actually contemplated a shotgun ambush for my former friend Zeke. Fortunately I used to take my shotgun completely apart when I was sober, so that when I got drunk I could never piece it back together. That was my version of arms control.

I kept drinking after losing the job and pretty much forgot about Zeke and the events of those times. They simply blended in with all the jobs and other friends I lost over the years.

A few years later I found my way through the doors of AA. It took me three more years to finally do a thorough inventory. With the sober guidance of a sponsor, I was able to see my part in the matter. My sponsor pointed out that I had actually lied about wanting a job, when all I really wanted was a steady source of drinking money. He helped me recognize how I betrayed a friend, using his name and reputation to get the job and relying on our friendship rather than hard work to keep it.

For years I'd used this incident to fuel my bitterness. Now, after sharing my Fifth Step, I understood that my resentment was due to prideful grandiosity and an ego-serving, one-sided view of the whole affair. It was painful to see myself in this light, more so because Zeke was only one of many people I used to continue my drinking. I pretended to be normal by blaming my insanity on them. This crazy thinking was so habitual in me that it didn't stop even after this hard look at myself, and I kept losing jobs until my fourth year of sobriety.

While I had humbly admitted that I owed Zeke amends, I suspected I would never make them. I satisfied myself by saying I would go through with it if ever the opportunity presented itself, but I wouldn't go looking for him. After all, he was as mean as I'd ever been and the prospect of apologizing to him only to receive scorn and contempt was not appealing.

I decided to discount the whole matter as nothing more than a disagreement between a couple of "lowlife drunks," not really deserving of attention or effort. Later I was shown that this was a selfish, dishonest attempt to avoid a painful meeting. It did not matter that Zeke was a "drunk." I was taking his inventory. Zeke's status or my judgment of his status should never have entered my thinking. The spiritual damage had been done and it needed to be cleaned up. I must be concerned with my side of the street.

And so it was that one afternoon, as I sat in one of my favorite AA meetings, guess who came in and sat down? Zeke. By now there was no question as to what I needed to do. As soon as the meeting ended I walked over and stuck out my hand.

"Zeke," I said, "it's been a while; it's good to see you here. I want to apologize to you for the way I acted on that job and for putting you in that position. I know you had to get me fired, and in hindsight, I would have done the same thing. You were good enough to get me that job, and I don't think I ever even thanked you for that. So I want to apologize to you, and if there's any way I can ever help you with your sobriety or anything else, I hope you will tell me!"

He stared at me for a moment, broke into a huge grin, gave me a big bear hug and said, "Well you are the last person I expected to run into. Thought you'd be dead by now. I just got out of treatment a couple of days ago. I could sure use a temporary sponsor!"

And with that, my former mortal enemy quickly became one of my best friends in AA. The long talks we had about God, about sobriety, about our childhoods, and about our troubles with all this character stuff, were some of the best times in those years of sobriety.

In trying to dissect everything that had preceded that meeting, I found myself once again profoundly awed by the wonder of our beautiful program and its ability to turn bitter enemies into the best of friends, make peace in families and restore ruined lives.

Zeke died with 10 years of sobriety. I knew from our many talks that his ambition was simply to live sober. For him that meant learning how to love, helping other alcoholics, trying to be a good man and serving the God of his understanding. I was a privileged witness to his abundant demonstration of all five.

James L.
Pegram, Tennessee

Open and Honest
February 1980

A few months after coming into the Fellowship of Alcoholics Anonymous, and solely under the motivation of fear, I compiled a list of those people to whom I judged I owed amends. At that stage of dryness, I felt compelled to do what the Steps suggested, lest I lose my precious sobriety. In retrospect, I find that attitude perfectly reasonable at that point.

On the list was a young woman, a professional colleague, who had been hurt by an action executed by me. She was unsure of the identity of the offender.

At every Eighth and Ninth Step meeting I attended during the following three years, I became increasingly aware that I must someday summon the courage to become honest and reveal my transgression to Lynne. Projection, a formerly favorite preoccupation, told me I undoubtedly would lose her companionship. False dependence told me I needed her as a friend. (Wanting is one thing; needing quite another.)

Lynne continued to be a good friend—especially generous with her invitations to social outings, her help, and her support whenever I permitted. Recently, when I knew she was about to perform yet one more act of affection, I became intensely uncomfortable. After 36 hours, I knew action was required to rid myself of the pain. I became willing to take the risk of losing her friendship. For my own good, I had to take Step Nine.

During the past eight months, I have become aware of the need to start liking myself. I realized that all other areas of my life hinged on the concept of self-worth. After repeated practice, I did progress in the direction of this goal. But I have learned in this challenging program that one is never finished. Sure enough, a dear friend drew to my attention that it was time to start loving myself. My original aversion to this idea has been removed, and I daily practice this new discipline.

It was through this mental exercise that I came to realize I had to be good to myself and stop dragging the past with me whenever I encountered Lynne. The friendship seemed doomed unless it could become a new relationship.

An empty conference room at nine on a Friday morning provided the setting for my revelation. Fortunately, the amends were graciously accepted. But curiously, tears from Lynne followed. She explained that she had been deeply hurt, not by my disclosure, but by my earlier withholding of the news that I was an alcoholic, had stopped drinking, and had embarked on a new life through AA.

I had held back, failing to share with her. The fear that Lynne might find the news repulsive and reject me as a friend caused my procrastination. She had not been able to discern why our conversations were short and lacking in meaning. Among other things, how does one explain traveling several evenings throughout each month around the state with various men if one's friend is unaware of AA speaker commitments?

Can it be that, at numerous discussion meetings, I actually told my group I was not a procrastinator and had no fears? Thank God, this is a program of mental growth and deepening awareness of self. Thank God, my eyes can open wider. Thank God, it is a gradual process. Thank God—acting through Bill W. and associates—for Steps Eight and Nine, which have healed wounds in an important relationship and have strengthened and enriched it.

How delightful to be open and honest! How delightful to be able to look Lynne squarely in the eyes and not feel that all-consuming, paralyzing guilt!

How delightful to grow up a little more! I almost called my sponsor to ask whether I should go ahead with the amends, but I knew the answer. I could use my sober mind and the pain in order to act as a mature woman and move in the direction my Higher Power was leading. I believed the leader of a recent meeting when he said that the intent of working Step Nine was to benefit me, not the other person, and that it would enable me to have a freer spirit as I continue to live my life. Now I know it. There is a difference.

B. F.
Meyersville, New Jersey

Ruff Love
(From Dear Grapevine)
March 2015

I just read the article "A Canine Step Nine"(March 2013). It took me six years of sobriety and reading that article for me to reflect on the harm caused to my dog, Snowflake, who saw me through my alcoholism and all my drunken moments. He's also been with me in sobriety. Today I am grateful I got to make a living amends to my dog, who showed me nothing but unconditional love. Two weeks after I read that issue, he had a stroke and I got to make my amends to him thanks to the perspective from that wonderful story. I barely left his side the weeks before he died and was able to return just a small bit of that unconditional love he gave me. I could never be grateful enough to the writer of that article and to Grapevine for publishing it. Since then my family has adopted a rescue dog and I continue to have the opportunity to live in that amends every day. As always, God places the right perspective at exactly the right time.

Shawna S.
Hopatcong, New Jersey

I'm Right and You're Wrong ... OK?
November 1996

After about a year and a half in the Fellowship of AA, I attended my usual six o'clock after-work meeting. I didn't know, as is often the case, that I was about to learn something very significant, something that would change the way I dealt with life.

It was early in December. I'd had a really lousy afternoon, and to cap things off, I'd gotten into an explicit shouting match on the telephone with a colleague over a place to hold a Christmas party for our department. My colleague (and friend) had offered, in August, to host the Christmas event in his division. Being the social chairman for the department, I hadn't readily accepted his generous offer in August. Now Christmas was just a few days off. I raised the issue of his August offer only to find him withholding, tentative and manipulative. He seemed to know and relish the fact that I was having difficulty in finding a place for this event. I really hadn't wanted to call him in the first place to ask for meeting space, but space for Christmas parties was really scarce. The conversation became heated and shouting ensued. I slammed down the phone and stormed around my office. How could he treat me this way? I hadn't done anything to him. Why should he be so belligerent? I was fuming, and rightly so, I thought.

I left work and headed for my six o'clock meeting. I arrived about 15 minutes early, still extremely angry and feeling greatly put-upon by my so-called colleague. An old-timer saw my plight and asked what was wrong. I told him that I had been unjustifiably wronged, manipulated and just plain mistreated. I stated that I needed to learn to be more assertive, to confront the other party, and be more honest about how I felt. The old-timer listened, paused, looked at the floor, and then reestablishing eye contact with me, said in a very gentle tone, "You know what you have to do, don't you?" I repeated that I needed to be more assertive and protect myself from this sort of thing—not let this happen to me again! The old-timer paused a second time, looked at the floor again, and said that I really needed to apologize to the other person. "Apologize to him!" I blurted out. "He should apologize to me. I didn't wrong him. He wronged me. He knew I was having a problem and he took advantage of me, my feelings and my situation. I didn't take advantage of him. He owes me an apology! I am the wronged person here."

My temporary mentor, with a touch of sarcasm in his voice, then said to me, "And you're going to be angry with him all night, aren't you?"

The meeting began and ended. I was still fuming. Neither the meeting nor the Lord's Prayer had shaken me out of the feelings of being wronged. I went home in that state of mind and continued fuming, but now another thought started bouncing around in my head. The old-timer had suggested to me that I needed to apologize to the other person. I try to do what's suggested, but this idea was 180 degrees from what I thought I needed to do. A war of ideas battled in my mind. My colleague had wronged me. Why should I apologize to him?

It took until about nine o'clock for me to decide to do what the old-timer had told me to do—apologize to the other person. I telephoned my colleague and began by saying that I wanted to apologize to him for the way I'd behaved earlier in the day. I told him I realized he couldn't have heard the things I'd wanted to say to him because of the way I was acting. No sooner than I was able to get out the apology, my colleague began lecturing me on how I should behave in a relationship. Immediately, my anger welled up inside me. But this time I restrained my anger and listened. When he was finished talking, I restated my apology and, instantaneously, my anger left me. I felt calm on the inside. We continued talking with one another. Later, as I got ready for bed, I realized that a big burden of uncomfortable feelings had been eased.

At the six o'clock meeting the following week, the old-timer asked me how I was doing. I replied that I'd done what he had suggested—I'd apologized to my colleague. It pleased him that I had done so and he asked me what I'd learned from the experience. I told him I'd learned that it's important not to get caught up in an argument as to who's right or wrong in a situation. I'd been so concerned with being right that I'd sacrificed how I was feeling. I've come to learn that when I'm upset or angry it's generally related to the fact that I have a need to be right and I'm not really focusing on my needs for peace and serenity. Apologizing or making amends now takes into account how I feel rather than my need to be right. Making amends or apologizing ultimately has little or nothing to do with who's right or wrong. It has to do with the fact that we're more concerned with our peace and serenity than with personal vindication. I also learned that the answer to my needs, especially in moments of high emotion, is usually radically different from what I think I need.

This experience occurred 10 years ago and my colleague and I are still friends.

Roger B.
Louisville, Kentucky

An Honest Amend
(From Dear Grapevine)
May 1997

I n November 1973, a kind and loving God told me I didn't have to be a drunk anymore. A few months later as I was studying the Twelve Steps, he reminded me that the time had come to begin to make amends. The thought of going to people to ask forgiveness and sincerely offer to make amends was initially scary, but I knew I was different now. I was honest and sincere, not just faking it, and I would gladly do whatever was needed to keep the peace of mind that had come with sobriety.

I knew the first person to seek out was Mel. He was not only a true friend but he also had been my boss during a period of time I'd made very difficult for him. So, nervous but at peace and ready, I called his office and asked to see him. He said to come right over.

I told Mel why I was there. Not only did my sobriety require it, but it was what I truly wanted to say: that I didn't know exactly how I had hurt him or the troubles I'd caused while I was drinking but that I was truly sorry for whatever that harm had been. I asked his forgiveness and said if there was anything I could do to make amends, I'd honestly and sincerely try to do it.

When I finished, there was a sense of peace and tranquility so pure it was almost unbelievable. Whatever he would ask of me, I would do with a happy heart.

Mel had leaned back in his chair while I was talking, listening intently and patiently. I stopped and waited for his response. He paused for a moment, then leaned forward across his desk, smiled and said, "Dick, you have already done it."

Richard H.
Burbank, California

A Letter from an Old Friend
Grapevine Online Exclusive
July 2011

I received the following response to a Ninth Step letter sent to a friend I had not corresponded with for over 20 years. She was the first person to suggest to me that I might have a problem with alcohol. It was important to me to locate her to make amends for my behavior.

I had been sober approximately four years when I finally found her. I explained the reason for my letter, that I was a grateful member of AA, made my apologies and offered to share my experience, strength and hope with anyone she might know who might also suffer from this disease. I really did not expect a response of any kind and was quite surprised to hear back from her.

With her permission I share this "anonymized" version of her response as it describes much more eloquently than I ever could the serious nature of our disease:

> *Hi Dave,*
>
> *First, let me tell you how much I admire your resolve to confront alcoholism. Congratulations on your upcoming fourth birthday, and may you have many more.*
>
> *Second, apologies accepted.*
>
> *You are fortunate indeed to be where you are. My husband was not so fortunate. I met him in 1987, a charming, hard-working, party-loving alcoholic, whom I married 6 years later. I believe alcohol was a significant factor in his death from suicide in 1997; he suffered depression and was intoxicated when he died. I wish I had known then what I know now about alcohol. I'd be much more willing to get help and less inclined to be angry that he was drinking all his money away. It's been a long, slow climb out of the grief and guilt that overwhelmed me for several years after he died.*
>
> *I cannot comprehend why some people experience an epiphany, as you did, and others leave this world without one. How different our lives would have been had we known to get help, or had there been an intervention, either divine or mortal. But those things, for whatever reason, did not happen.*
>
> *Great to hear from you, and keep up the recovery.*

I can't describe the emotions I experienced as I read this note. We all know that alcoholism touches the lives of everyone the alcoholic comes in contact with, some more tangibly than others, some more tragically than others.

In my case I believe my Higher Power intervened in my life and showed me the way to AA. Any epiphany I may have had was the direct result of working the Steps, developing a personal relationship with my Higher Power and paying attention to others who shared their experience, strength and hope with me. I hope that these words will resonate with another alcoholic so that they may find the serenity in their life that I have found in mine.

Dave B.

The Twelve Steps

1. We admitted we were powerless over alcohol—that our lives had become unmanageable.

2. Came to believe that a Power greater than ourselves could restore us to sanity.

3. Made a decision to turn our will and our lives over to the care of God *as we understood Him.*

4. Made a searching and fearless moral inventory of ourselves.

5. Admitted to God, to ourselves, and to another human being the exact nature of our wrongs.

6. Were entirely ready to have God remove all these defects of character.

7. Humbly asked Him to remove our shortcomings.

8. Made a list of all persons we had harmed, and became willing to make amends to them all.

9. Made direct amends to such people wherever possible, except when to do so would injure them or others.

10. Continued to take personal inventory and when we were wrong promptly admitted it.

11. Sought through prayer and meditation to improve our conscious contact with God *as we understood Him,* praying only for knowledge of His will for us and the power to carry that out.

12. Having had a spiritual awakening as the result of these steps, we tried to carry this message to alcoholics, and to practice these principles in all our affairs.

The Twelve Traditions

1. Our common welfare should come first; personal recovery depends upon A.A. unity.
2. For our group purpose there is but one ultimate authority—a loving God as He may express Himself in our group conscience. Our leaders are but trusted servants; they do not govern.
3. The only requirement for A.A. membership is a desire to stop drinking.
4. Each group should be autonomous except in matters affecting other groups or A.A. as a whole.
5. Each group has but one primary purpose—to carry its message to the alcoholic who still suffers.
6. An A.A. group ought never endorse, finance or lend the A.A. name to any related facility or outside enterprise, lest problems of money, property and prestige divert us from our primary purpose.
7. Every A.A. group ought to be fully self-supporting, declining outside contributions.
8. Alcoholics Anonymous should remain forever nonprofessional, but our service centers may employ special workers.
9. A.A., as such, ought never be organized; but we may create service boards or committees directly responsible to those they serve.
10. Alcoholics Anonymous has no opinion on outside issues; hence the A.A. name ought never be drawn into public controversy.
11. Our public relations policy is based on attraction rather than promotion; we need always maintain personal anonymity at the level of press, radio and films.
12. Anonymity is the spiritual foundation of all our traditions, ever reminding us to place principles before personalities.

Alcoholics Anonymous

AA's program of recovery is fully set forth in its basic text, *Alcoholics Anonymous* (commonly known as the Big Book), now in its Fourth Edition, as well as in *Twelve Steps and Twelve Traditions, Living Sober,* and other books. Information on AA can also be found on AA's website at WWW.AA.ORG, or by writing to:

Alcoholics Anonymous
Box 459
Grand Central Station
New York, NY 10163

For local resources, check your local telephone directory under "Alcoholics Anonymous." Four pamphlets, "This is A.A.," "Is A.A. For You?," "44 Questions," and "A Newcomer Asks" are also available from AA.

AA Grapevine

AA Grapevine is AA's international monthly journal, published continuously since its first issue in June 1944. The AA pamphlet on AA Grapevine describes its scope and purpose this way: "As an integral part of Alcoholics Anonymous since 1944, the Grapevine publishes articles that reflect the full diversity of experience and thought found within the A.A. Fellowship, as does La Viña, the bimonthly Spanish-language magazine, first published in 1996. No one viewpoint or philosophy dominates their pages, and in determining content, the editorial staff relies on the principles of the Twelve Traditions."

In addition to magazines, AA Grapevine, Inc. also produces books, eBooks, audiobooks, and other items. It also offers a Grapevine Online subscription, which includes: new stories weekly, AudioGrapevine (the audio version of the magazine), Grapevine Story Archive (the entire collection of Grapevine articles), and the current issue of Grapevine and La Viña in HTML format. For more information on AA Grapevine, or to subscribe to any of these, please visit the magazine's website at WWW.AAGRAPEVINE.ORG or write to:

AA Grapevine, Inc.
475 Riverside Drive
New York, NY 10115